CUPCAKE
COOKBOOK
FOR KIDS

CUPCAKE
COOKBOOK
FOR KIDS

Charity Curley Mathews
founder of Foodlets.com

PHOTOGRAPHY BY LAURA FLIPPEN

R

ROCKRIDGE
PRESS

For general information on our other products and services or to obtain technical support, please contact our Customer Care Department within the United States at (866) 744-2665, or outside the United States at (510) 253-0500.

Rockridge Press publishes its books in a variety of electronic and print formats. Some content that appears in print may not be available in electronic books, and vice versa.

TRADEMARKS: Rockridge Press and the Rockridge Press logo are trademarks or registered trademarks of Callisto Media Inc. and/or its affiliates, in the United States and other countries, and may not be used without written permission. All other trademarks are the property of their respective owners. Rockridge Press is not associated with any product or vendor mentioned in this book.

Interior and Cover Designer: Liz Cosgrove
Art Producer: Hannah Dickerson
Editor: Laura Apperson
Production Editor: Ruth Sakata Corley

Photography © 2020 Laura Flippen

Decorative patterns and icons courtesy of Shutterstock

Interior author photo courtesy of Colleen Chrzanowski

ISBN: Print 978-1-64739-269-7
eBook 978-1-64739-270-3

R0

For Violet,
George, Estelle, and
Phoebe, my own
tiny bakers

contents

Gather 'round the Campfire Cupcakes, page 88

introduction

Welcome to your very own book all about cupcakes!

I have four kids who love baking cupcakes as much as you do. While making this book, they tried every single recipe, and I promise, we devoured them all. Now it's your turn.

In chapter 1, you'll learn everything you need to know to be a master cupcake baker. Packed with terms, tips, and tricks, this chapter will teach you everything from safety lessons to decorating techniques you'll love.

Chapter 2 starts with classics like rich chocolate, vanilla, carrot cake, and red velvet cupcakes. If you're a beginner, this is a great chapter to start with.

In chapter 3, you'll find cupcakes with creamy fillings, where every bite includes a surprise. These recipes are a bit more advanced, and you may need an adult to help, but the results are worth it!

Baking for a special occasion? That's where the adorable decorating ideas from chapters 4 and 5 come in. In chapter 4, you'll find birthday favorites, including Melting Ice-Cream Cones (page 86), Fresh Fish with Colorful Candy Scales (page 84), Marshmallow Flowers (page 82), and Bears on the Beach (page 96). You're also set for every season of the year and holiday: heart-shaped cupcakes to make Valentine's Day even sweeter (page 104), chocolate Springtime Bird Nests (page 108), and, of course, we have the winter holidays covered (page 119). But that's just skimming the surface. Flip through these pages and bookmark your favorite ideas to try all year long.

Ready to get rolling?

Let's dig in.

chapter 1

HOW TO BAKE THE PERFECT CUPCAKE

With just a few simple techniques, you'll be able to perfect your cupcake skills and dazzle friends and family for any celebration.

GETTING COMFORTABLE IN THE KITCHEN

Every project in the kitchen starts (and ends) with one thing: cleaning. Wash your hands with soap and scrub them for at least 20 seconds before rinsing, then dry your hands with a fresh towel. I also like to clear off the counters and wipe them down. Then it's time to get organized:

1. When I bake with my kids, we always wear aprons. It helps keep our clothes clean and makes us feel official.

2. Set up a garbage bowl to toss eggshells, butter wrappers, and the like so you won't have to walk across the kitchen to throw anything away.

3. Grab a wet rag for wiping sticky fingers at the counter.

4. Read the whole recipe—from start to finish—before you begin baking. Make sure you understand all the steps and the order to do them.

5. Gather all the ingredients and materials you'll need. It's better to find out that you are out of eggs before you start baking, rather than halfway through. Plus, you'll save time not having to run repeatedly to the refrigerator and pantry. French chefs call this *mise en place* (meez on plahss), which means "everything in its place."

Now we're ready to bake.

ESSENTIAL CUPCAKE SKILLS

Master cupcake baking techniques with these simple skills. All it takes is practice.

🧁 Baking 101

Baking is actually science! When you combine the right ingredients and then apply heat, the whole recipe transforms from liquid to solid. These tips will help you become a better baker.

BE AN EXPERT BAKER
SAFETY FIRST

The kitchen is a delicious place, but it can also be dangerous. Always have an adult in the room while you're baking. From using the oven (turning it on and off, putting pans in and taking them out), to microwaving and measuring properly, the more supervision you get, the better your skills will get—and the safer you'll be.

And always be smart about food safety. Food poisoning occurs when you eat food that's been contaminated, typically by bacteria. It is real, and trust me, you don't want to experience it. But don't worry! Food poisoning is generally preventable with a few smart moves:

1. *Really* wash your hands before you bake. Soap up and sing the ABC song while rubbing your hands together for at least 20 seconds. Rinse well with warm water and dry your hands with a fresh towel.

2. Many recipes in this book call for butter that's warmed to room temperature. It's safe to let butter warm up on the counter (or in the microwave for 10 seconds), but never leave raw ingredients out for more than 4 hours.

3. Cook your cupcakes thoroughly. Your cupcakes should look firm and spring back when you touch the tops. Ask an adult to confirm.

4. Store your cupcakes on the counter in a covered dish or tray for up to 2 days. After that, move any leftovers to the refrigerator, where they'll stay fresh for about 1 week.

Measuring

There are three basic tools for measuring:

1. Glass measuring cup with a spout
2. Metal or plastic measuring cups with flat tops
3. Measuring spoons

Use a **glass measuring cup** with a spout to measure liquids, such as oil, milk, and water. Place the measuring cup on the counter. Bend down so your eyes are in line with the liquid you are measuring. See how there's a dip in the center? Line up the bottom of the dip with the mark you need. For example, if you need 1 cup of water, the bottom of the dip should line up with the 1-cup mark.

Regular metal or plastic measuring cups work for all dry ingredients, including flour and sugar, but the technique for measuring each ingredient is different. Sugar can be scooped straight out of the bag with the measuring cup and leveled off with the back of a butter knife. But, when measuring flour, you need to be more precise to avoid accidentally adding too much flour. Use a large spoon to scoop flour into the measuring cup, then level it off with the straight edge of a butter knife before adding the flour to your recipe.

Every stick of butter comes premeasured, with tablespoons and cups labeled right on the wrapper (1 stick = 8 tablespoons, or ½ cup). Use a table knife to cut the butter at the line you need.

Mixing Batter

A surprisingly important part of baking is using air to keep your cakes light. Use the following methods to keep your cakes from becoming heavy:

Creaming: Many recipes start with creaming the butter. This means placing the butter (and often the sugar) in a bowl and beating for about 3 minutes until fluffy. The added air makes your batter light and helps distribute the sugar evenly once the rest of the ingredients are added.

Folding: Folding means to add an ingredient without beating out all the air you just added! Using a silicone spatula, gently slice down to the bottom of the bowl, then over, up, and across the top again—like you're making the shape of a circle.

Mixing until just combined: Once flour is added to any mixture, the chances of overmixing your batter become real. Think of how you knead bread. The more you work it, the firmer your dough gets. That's because gluten develops with action. For cakes (and cupcakes), we want the opposite. Once you see your flour start to disappear in the mixture, turn off the mixer and use your silicone spatula to stir gently one or two last times.

Preparing the Pan

Preparing your pan is one of the most important steps in baking. You can slide one paper or silicone cupcake liner into each muffin cup or use a paper towel to smear butter into each cup. Alternatively, you can spray your pan with nonstick cooking spray. Never pour cupcake batter into a pan that hasn't been prepped. You won't be able to get the cupcakes out!

Melting Butter

Ask an adult to help you heat butter in a microwave-safe bowl. Heat on High power for 20 seconds, stir, and then repeat in short increments as needed.

Cracking and Separating Eggs

1. If a recipe calls for an egg, crack it lightly on the side of the bowl before pouring it in. If an eggshell drops into the bowl with the egg, use half an eggshell to fish it out.

2. These are the simplest ways to separate egg yolks and egg whites:

   - Crack an egg into a bowl. Gently use your (clean) fingers to scoop up the yolk and let the whites fall through your fingers.

   - Working over a bowl, pour the yolk from one half of the shell to the other, repeating as necessary until all the whites fall into the bowl and just the yolk remains in the shell.

Bringing Butter and Eggs to Room Temperature

Cold butter and eggs won't combine well with other ingredients. Both can be left on a counter for up to 4 hours to warm to room temperature. Need a faster method? Butter can be warmed in the microwave: Heat it on High power for 10 seconds at a time until the butter is softened but has not melted. Eggs can be placed in a bowl of warm water for 5 to 10 minutes.

🧁 Using Sharp Tools

It takes practice (and courage) to get good at slicing and dicing, so always ask an adult to help with these steps.

Practicing Good Knife Skills

Sharp knives are often necessary in the kitchen, so it's important to follow a few specific rules for safety.

- Always use a small paring knife or plastic child-safe knife.
- Curl under the tips of your fingers holding the food to protect them from the knife while you are chopping.
- Use a clean cutting board. If the board is slipping, place a damp kitchen towel underneath to keep it stable.
- When cutting, place the fruit or vegetable flat-side down so it's more stable.
- Take your time. Accidents are more likely to happen when you rush.

Graters and Peelers

Some cupcake recipes call for fresh zest. You'll need a zester, a fine-toothed grater, or the smallest holes of a box grater.

1. Wash your fruit first.

2. Position the grater over a cutting board, then carefully rub the edge of your fruit back and forth against the grater.

3. Stop grating when you get to the white part of the fruit—that's called the pith and it tastes bitter—and always be careful of your fingers and knuckles.

🧁 Using the Oven

Everyone knows a hot oven can be dangerous. Always use oven mitts and never, ever operate the oven without an adult in the room.

Here are some other practical tips for using your oven with the most success:

Preheat the oven. Always preheat the oven right when you start baking; it takes at least 10 minutes to get to the temperature you need. If you start baking cupcakes when the oven is halfway to the temperature needed, your cupcakes won't be ready when the timer beeps. Plus, temperature affects how your cupcakes rise and whether the batter will be cooked.

Use the center rack. To ensure your cupcakes are heated from all sides, position your pan on the center rack.

Rotate the pan. Because most ovens don't cook evenly, I like to rotate the pans halfway through the cooking time. Always have an adult help with this step and use oven mitts.

Keep the oven door closed. Other than to rotate the pan, don't open the oven door unless you need to take the cupcakes out. Want to check on them? Turn on the oven light. Every time you open the door, warmth escapes and the cooking time changes, as the oven has to heat up again.

Think ahead. Have your oven mitts at the ready so you aren't scrambling when you need to take your cupcakes out of the oven—and clear a safe, flat place for the hot pan to cool off (ask an adult to help).

🧁 Decorating Techniques and Tips

You'll find two whole chapters devoted to making your cupcakes gorgeous (chapter 4: Birthday Party Ideas, page 75, and chapter 5: Holiday Ideas, page 103). Plus, you'll find 10 recipes for frosting in chapter 6.

This is what the pros do to make their cupcakes gorgeous:

Warm the frosting. If you've made the frosting ahead, place it in the bowl of your stand mixer and mix it on medium speed for about 2 minutes to soften it before decorating your cupcakes.

No piping bag? No problem. If you love the swirly look of frosting but don't have professional tools, use a regular resealable bag and cut off one corner with scissors. *Ta-da!* Your own DIY piping tool.

Keep the sprinkles contained. When my kids decorate with sprinkles, I set out rimmed baking sheets for each child to use as a work space. Wayward sprinkles get trapped before they hit the kitchen floor, plus everyone has their own designated work area.

Decorating with a crowd? Put the frosting and sprinkles on a lazy Susan to spin around, offering each baker a chance to use everything. Or set up painters' palettes with one cupcake in the center and a different kind of candy, crushed cookies, or sprinkles in each divot. This is especially fun for parties.

How to Frost Your Cupcakes

Here are my two favorite techniques for frosting cupcakes:

1. **Smooth top:** Place a big spoonful of frosting on top of your cupcake (or use an ice-cream scoop with a spring release). With a table knife or offset spatula, level the top. Then tilt the spatula and run it all the way around the edges of the frosting so you end up with a thick layer of frosting with a flat top. This is the perfect way to serve a simple frosted cupcake or use it as a blank canvas for the decorating ideas you'll find in chapters 4 and 5.

2. **Piping:** Have an adult help you prepare a piping bag with a large round tip. Fold the edges of the bag halfway down and use a silicone spatula to fill the bag with frosting. Fold the edges of the bag back up, twist the top of the bag to secure it, then squeeze down on the frosting. Move your hands in a circular pattern while squeezing to make a swirl. This works best for cupcakes you plan to serve plain or with one extra decorative touch like a piece of chocolate or fruit.

KNOW YOUR FROSTING

In this book we use four different types of frosting:

Buttercream: Traditional buttercream—including my recipes for Peanut Butter Frosting (page 132), Chocolate (page 135), Vanilla (page 128), and Fruity Buttercream (page 129)—is made by combining butter with powdered sugar and milk until fluffy. Other flavors can be added, such as cocoa powder, vanilla, lemon zest, jam, and so on.

Cream cheese: As the name suggests, Cream Cheese Frosting (page 131) is made with full-fat cream cheese, butter, and powdered sugar. Extra ingredients like coconut can be added, too (see page 131).

Glaze: Glaze, including Lemon (page 133) and Chocolate (page 134), is runnier than regular frosting and is meant to drizzle on top of cupcakes. Let it firm up a bit before serving.

Whipped cream: Instead of plain whipped cream that would melt if left at room temperature, my Whipped Cream Frosting (page 130) uses a secret ingredient: instant pudding. The gelatin in the pudding helps the frosting set, plus adds a delicious punch of flavor.

Remember, always store frosting in the refrigerator. If you're preparing frosting ahead of time, refrigerate it in an airtight container for up to 2 weeks. When ready to use, take it out of the refrigerator 20 to 30 minutes before frosting, and let it come *almost* to room temperature. Most frosting spreads best when it's slightly cooler than room temperature (so it doesn't melt). Need more time? Freeze your frosting in an airtight container for up to 2 months. Let the frosting thaw and stir it before using.

KEEPING A CUPCAKE KITCHEN

Making cupcakes is a lot like baking cakes, using many of the same techniques, tools, and ingredients. With a few special techniques, you can turn out perfect cupcakes every time.

🧁 Cupcake Equipment

- **Cupcake liners:** Made of paper or silicone, the options for cupcake liners are endless. Just keep in mind, most paper liners won't show up as brightly once the cupcakes are baked. If you have your heart set on a special design, add a second liner to the cupcakes after they are baked and once they're cooled.

- **Ice-cream scoop with spring release:** To measure batter evenly, I like to use a #20 ice-cream scoop with a thumb spring. If that's not possible, use a ¼-cup measuring cup and scrape out the batter with a silicone spatula.

- **Measuring cups and spoons:** Bakers need a standard set of dry measuring cups and spoons plus a liquid glass measuring cup with a spout.

- **Metal sifter:** This tool has a finely woven metal screen used to remove clumps from dry ingredients like flour and baking powder.

- **Mixing bowls:** Because baking is science, many recipes require mixing dry ingredients (like flour) separately from the wet ingredients (like milk), so you'll need up to three bowls.

- **Silicone spatula:** This tool is best for folding and scraping down the sides of mixing bowls.

- **Stand mixer:** When baking with kids, I like a stand mixer with the paddle attachment, but a large bowl using electric beaters works, too.

- **Standard muffin pan:** Every recipe in this book makes one dozen regular cupcakes, so you'll need a pan with 12 cups. Aluminum pans are the most common and easiest to use. I don't recommend silicone pans because they're too unstable for little hands to handle safely.

- **Wire rack:** This flat rack made of woven metal with raised legs is designed to allow airflow from all sides so baked goods cool properly.

🧁 Decorating Tools and Special Ingredients

- **Food coloring:** Natural food coloring can be found online or at specialty baking stores.

- **Kitchen scissors:** For cutting candy and marshmallows, clean and sharp scissors are a must.

- **Offset spatula:** Long and skinny with a rounded edge, this tool helps spread frosting evenly. If you don't have one, a butter knife makes a good substitute.

- **Piping bag and tips:** Made of plastic, piping bags are tools professionals use to squeeze frosting onto cupcakes in special shapes. Using a piping bag is an advanced skill, but don't worry, it's optional for all the ideas in this book.

- **Sprinkles:** Many of our decorating ideas include sprinkles, and all of them can be found in the baking aisle of any grocery store.

Cupcake Staple Ingredients

All the ingredients called for in these recipes and decorating ideas can be found at the grocery store, with the exception of natural food coloring, which may be ordered online or purchased at a specialty baking store.

In Your Refrigerator

- **Large eggs:** All the recipes in this book call for large eggs. For best results, remove eggs from the refrigerator 30 minutes before using so they can come to room temperature (or set eggs in a bowl of warm water for 5 to 10 minutes to warm).

- **Unsalted butter:** All the recipes in this book call for unsalted butter. Butter should be refrigerated unless being softened for immediate use. To soften butter, leave it on the counter for up to 4 hours, or microwave on High power in 10-second increments until soft.

- **Whole milk or buttermilk:** These recipes were tested using regular dairy milk. When a recipe calls for buttermilk and you don't have any available, just add vinegar or freshly squeezed lemon juice to dairy milk and let sit for about 5 minutes. Bam! Homemade buttermilk.

In Your Pantry

- **All-purpose flour:** We use all-purpose flour for the recipes in this book. Store flour in an airtight container where it'll stay fresh for up to 1 year.

- **Baking powder:** More powerful than baking soda, baking powder adds tiny bubbles to a batter, causing it to rise. Replace your baking powder every season for best results.

- **Baking soda:** Also known as sodium bicarbonate, baking soda produces tiny bubbles in the batter to help it rise. Stored in an airtight container, it'll keep for up to 1 year.

- **Chocolate chips:** Semisweet is the most common flavor of these small pieces of chocolate, but you can find dark, milk, and even white chocolate and butterscotch chips in almost every grocery store.

- **Fine salt:** Fine salt (not coarse salt) is best for these recipes. Table salt, iodized salt, sea salt, or kosher are all good choices.

- **Granulated sugar:** This is regular crystalized white sugar (often just listed as sugar). Store in an airtight container to prevent hardening.

- **Powdered sugar:** Also known as confectioners' sugar, this is very finely ground granulated sugar with cornstarch added to prevent lumps. You can make your own powdered sugar: In a blender, combine 1 cup of granulated sugar with 1 tablespoon of cornstarch and blend for about 3 minutes.

- **Sweetened shredded coconut:** This is grated coconut with added sugar. Finely shredded is preferred but any size shred will work. Store unused leftovers in an airtight container for up to 6 months.

- **Unsweetened cocoa powder:** Unsweetened cocoa powder is made from ground cocoa seeds. It's pure chocolate that tastes bitter on its own.

- **Vinegar:** A type of naturally occurring acid, vinegar is used to add tang or help produce air bubbles to make cupcakes rise.

Decorating Delights

From fun ideas for sprinkles and melted s'mores (minus the camp-fire) to marshmallow flowers and tiny fish with candy scales, you'll learn how to transform plain cupcakes into the centerpiece of any occasion! Here are the decorating ingredients I like to have on hand:

- Candy
- Chocolate chips and bars
- Food coloring
- Marshmallows
- Sprinkles
- Graham crackers (and Teddy bear–shaped grahams)

WANT TO MAKE MINI CUPCAKES?

You can transform all the recipes in this book into mini cupcakes by making two adjustments:

1. You'll need a special 24-cup mini-cupcake pan.

2. Reduce the baking time by half. For example, if a recipe calls for a 16-minute bake time, start checking your mini cupcakes at 8 minutes. When you can (carefully) press down on the top of a cupcake and it springs back, your minis are done.

HOW TO USE THIS BOOK

From simple cupcake recipes to fluffy frosting and *tons* of decorating ideas, you'll be able to create 40 different combinations of delicious treats with this book. Every cupcake recipe makes a dozen cupcakes and comes with a recommendation for frosting, but, as the baker, you always get to pick your favorite ways to mix and match. Just turn the pages until you find what you want.

All the recipes in this book are perfect for cooks ages 8 and up. To help you identify the best recipes to start with, we've rated each with one, two, or three cupcakes:

EASY = Difficulty 1

These recipes involve the most basic baking steps, perfect for beginners. Mix your ingredients, put them in the pan, and bake in the oven. You'll find simple recipes like Chocolate Cupcakes (page 31) and Strawberry Cupcakes (page 23).

MODERATE = Difficulty 2

These recipes move to the next skill level, including steps like grating carrots, zesting fruit, or separating eggs.

HARD = Difficulty 3

These recipes involve steps that require a little more care. For example, you might fill cupcakes or use a fancy decorating technique.

Each recipe also includes a list of ingredients and kitchen tools you'll need, as well as step-by-step instructions. Most recipes require the help of an adult—and these are all called out in the instructions or with an "Ask an Adult" tip at the end of the recipe.

If you can't eat nuts, look for recipes with the label "Nut-Free." All the recipes are vegetarian but none are gluten-free.

At the end of each recipe you'll find a fun fact, piece of advice, or tip for making a different version. For the cupcakes that do not have a photo in this book, visit Foodlets.com/cupcakes to find it online.

Ready to bake? Let's do it!

chapter 2

CUPCAKE CLASSICS

From rich chocolate to creamy vanilla, pumpkin, and strawberry, these crowd-pleasing flavors are perfect for any occasion.

Need more photos? Visit my website at Foodlets.com/cupcakes for pictures of each recipe.

COCONUT CUPCAKES WITH CREAM CHEESE–COCONUT FROSTING

Coconuts come from palm trees in tropical areas such as Indonesia and the Philippines, but you won't have to go far to enjoy these delicious coconut cupcakes. With powdery white centers and fluffy white frosting, these treats are perfect for a party with a beach or winter wonderland theme.

MAKES 12 CUPCAKES	PREP TIME 30 MINUTES	BAKE TIME 20 MINUTES

Nonstick cooking spray (optional)

12 tablespoons (1½ sticks) unsalted butter, at room temperature, plus more for preparing the pan (optional)

1 cup sugar

1½ cups all-purpose flour

1 teaspoon baking powder

½ teaspoon baking soda

½ teaspoon fine salt

3 large eggs

2 teaspoons pure vanilla extract

½ cup buttermilk (see Super Baker tip)

7 ounces (half a 14-ounce bag) sweetened shredded coconut

1 batch Cream Cheese–Coconut Frosting (page 131)

TOOLS

Standard 12-cup muffin pan

Cupcake liners (optional)

Measuring cups and spoons

Stand mixer fitted with paddle attachment or large bowl and electric beaters

Silicone spatula

Mixing bowls

Whisk or fork

Small bowl

#20 ice-cream scoop with spring release

Oven mitts
Wire rack
Knife or offset spatula

1. **Preheat the oven.** Set the oven to 325°F. Line a muffin pan with paper liners, or grease the inside of each cup with cooking spray or butter (see page 5).

2. **Cream the butter.** In the bowl of a stand mixer fitted with the paddle attachment, or a large bowl using electric beaters, cream together the butter and sugar on medium speed for about 3 minutes until fluffy, stopping partway through to scrape down the sides of the bowl with a spatula. Once the butter is fluffy, stop the mixer.

3. **Mix the dry ingredients.** In another large bowl, combine the flour, baking powder, baking soda, and salt. Using a whisk or a fork, stir about 20 times to combine well. Set aside.

4. **Mix the wet ingredients.** Crack 1 egg into a small bowl (if you get any shell in it, see page 5 for tips on easily removing it). Add the egg to the butter mixture. Mix on medium speed for 1 minute. Stop the mixer and use a spatula to scrape down the sides of the bowl. Repeat with the remaining 2 eggs, mixing for 1 minute after each addition. Add the vanilla and mix for 1 minute.

Stop the mixer and use the spatula to scrape down the sides of the bowl.

5. **Add the dry ingredients to the wet ingredients.** Pour half the flour mixture into the butter mixture. Mix on low speed for 10 seconds. Add ¼ cup of buttermilk. Mix on low speed for 10 seconds. Stop the mixer and use the spatula to scrape down the sides of the bowl. Add the remaining flour mixture and remaining ¼ cup of buttermilk, mixing for 10 seconds between each addition. Using the spatula, scrape down the sides of the bowl. Stir the batter a few more times just until you can't see any flour.

6. **Add the coconut.** Using a spatula, fold (stir down, over, and up again, repeating in a circle) in the coconut until the batter is fully mixed, about 10 times.

7. **Fill the pan.** Use an ice-cream scoop to divide the batter evenly among the prepared cups, filling each about three-quarters full.

8. **Bake.** Carefully place the pan onto the center rack of the preheated oven. Bake for 18 to 20 minutes, rotating the pan halfway through the baking time (use oven mitts!) so your cupcakes bake evenly. The cupcakes are ready when you can press on the top of them with your finger and the cake springs back (ask an adult to help).

CONTINUED ON NEXT PAGE

9. **Let cool.** Remove the pan from the oven (use oven mitts!) and place it on a wire rack. Let the cupcakes cool in the pan for 10 minutes. Once they're cool enough to touch, remove the cupcakes from the pan and transfer them to the wire rack to cool completely, about 1 hour.

10. **Make the frosting.** While the cupcakes are cooling, make the cream cheese–coconut frosting following the directions on page 131.

11. **Frost the cupcakes.** Once the cupcakes are completely cooled, use a knife or offset spatula to spread an even layer of frosting on top of each cupcake.

Decorating Tip: Ask an adult to help: Toast a little coconut in an even layer on a baking sheet at 325°F for 5 to 10 minutes. Roll the edges of your frosted cupcakes in the golden coconut flakes. Or find edible flowers at stores like Whole Foods or online. The white frosting looks gorgeous with a pop of pink or red color.

Super Baker: No buttermilk? Make your own by adding ½ tablespoon of white vinegar to ½ cup of regular milk and letting it sit for a few minutes. Or substitute an equal amount of plain yogurt.

PUMPKIN CUPCAKES WITH WHIPPED CREAM FROSTING

Move over, pumpkin pie. You're going to fall hard for these pumpkin cupcakes topped with dreamy whipped cream frosting! Full of zesty cinnamon and tangy sour cream, these are soft and moist and, best of all, easy to make. You can even decorate these with a handful of chocolate chips or toasted walnuts to make them extra special.

MAKES	PREP TIME	BAKE TIME	
12 CUPCAKES	**25** MINUTES	**20** MINUTES	NUT-FREE

🔄 **Change It Up:** No sour cream? Substitute an equal amount of plain yogurt.

🍥 **Decorating Tip:** Give your guests a clue about what's inside! Perch a candy pumpkin atop the big swirl of frosting.

Nonstick cooking spray, or unsalted butter for preparing the pan (optional)

⅔ cup packed light brown sugar

½ cup olive oil

1 cup pure pumpkin puree (about half a 15-ounce can)

½ cup full-fat sour cream

2 large eggs

1½ cups all-purpose flour

2 teaspoons ground cinnamon

2 teaspoons baking powder

1½ teaspoons pumpkin pie spice, or 1 teaspoon ground ginger plus ½ teaspoon ground nutmeg

1 teaspoon baking soda

½ teaspoon fine salt

1 batch Whipped Cream Frosting (page 130)

TOOLS

Standard 12-cup muffin pan

Cupcake liners (optional)

Measuring cups and spoons

Stand mixer fitted with paddle attachment or large bowl and electric beaters

Small bowl

Silicone spatula

Sifter

#20 ice-cream scoop with spring release

CONTINUED ON NEXT PAGE

PUMPKIN CUPCAKES WITH WHIPPED CREAM FROSTING

CONTINUED

Oven mitts
Wire rack
Knife or offset spatula

1. Preheat the oven. Set the oven to 350°F. Line a muffin pan with paper liners, or grease the inside of each muffin cup with cooking spray or butter (see page 5).

2. Mix the dry ingredients. In the bowl of a stand mixer fitted with the paddle attachment, or a large bowl using electric beaters, combine the brown sugar, oil, pumpkin, and sour cream. Mix on medium speed for about 2 minutes until fluffy.

3. Add the eggs. Crack 1 egg into a small bowl (if you get any shell in it, see page 5 for tips on easily removing it). Add the egg to your sugar mixture. Mix on medium speed for 1 minute. Stop the mixer and use a spatula to scrape down the sides of the bowl. Repeat with the remaining egg, beating again for 1 minute.

4. Sift the dry ingredients. Remove the bowl from the mixer stand. Place a sifter over the bowl. Add the flour, cinnamon, baking powder, pumpkin pie spice, baking soda, and salt to the sifter. Gently shake the sifter to move all the ingredients into the bowl. Using the spatula, gently fold (stir down, over, and up again, repeating in a circle) the flour

mixture into the pumpkin mixture until fully incorporated.

5. Fill the pan. Using an ice-cream scoop, divide the batter evenly among the prepared cups, filling each about three-quarters full.

6. Bake. Carefully place the pan onto the center rack of the preheated oven. Bake for 18 to 20 minutes, rotating the pan halfway through baking (use oven mitts!) so your cupcakes bake evenly. The cupcakes are ready when you can press on the top of them with your finger and the cake springs back (ask an adult to help).

7. Let cool. Remove the pan from the oven (use oven mitts!) and place on a wire rack. Let the cupcakes cool in the pan for 10 minutes. Once they're cool enough to touch, remove the cupcakes from the pan and transfer them to the wire rack to cool completely, about 1 hour.

8. Make the frosting. While the cupcakes are cooling, make the whipped cream frosting following the directions on page 130.

9. Frost the cupcakes. Once the cupcakes are completely cooled, use a knife or offset spatula to spread an even layer of frosting on top of each cupcake.

STRAWBERRY CUPCAKES WITH STRAWBERRY FROSTING

Nothing says spring like a strawberry cupcake! And although they're in season at this time, fresh (or frozen) strawberries are just too juicy to work well in this recipe. But don't worry. We've got a secret weapon: strawberry jam! Already sweetened, it's thick enough to add flavor without making your cupcakes soggy. Do keep a dozen beautiful fresh strawberries on hand for decoration. They're especially pretty if you slice them a few times then fan out the pieces, all perched atop a mountain of pink strawberry frosting.

Nonstick cooking spray (optional)

6 tablespoons (¾ stick) unsalted butter, at room temperature, plus more for preparing the pan (optional)

¼ cup strawberry jam

6 tablespoons (a bit more than ⅓ cup) whole milk

2 teaspoons pure vanilla extract

2 large eggs

6 tablespoons sugar

1⅛ cups all-purpose flour

2 teaspoons baking powder

½ teaspoon fine salt

1 batch Fruity Buttercream with strawberry jam (page 129)

TOOLS

Standard 12-cup muffin pan

Cupcake liners (optional)

Measuring cups and spoons

Large bowl

Small bowl

Whisk

Stand mixer fitted with paddle attachment or large bowl with electric beaters

Silicone spatula

Sifter

#20 ice-cream scoop with spring release

Oven mitts

Wire rack

Knife or offset spatula

MAKES	PREP TIME	BAKE TIME	
12 CUPCAKES	**25** MINUTES	**20** MINUTES	**NUT-FREE**

 **Change It Up:** Add the zest of 1 lemon to your batter. Or fold (using a spatula, stir down, over, and up again, repeating in a circle) in a handful of mini chocolate chips in step 4.

CONTINUED ON NEXT PAGE

STRAWBERRY CUPCAKES WITH STRAWBERRY FROSTING

CONTINUED

1. Preheat the oven. Set the oven to 350°F. Line a muffin pan with paper liners, or grease the inside of each cup with cooking spray or butter (see page 5).

2. Mix the wet ingredients. In a large bowl, combine the strawberry jam, milk, and vanilla. Crack 1 egg into a small bowl (if you get any shell in it, see page 5 for tips on easily removing it). Add the egg to your jam mixture. Repeat with the remaining egg, then whisk until the eggs are fully incorporated.

3. Cream the butter. In the bowl of a stand mixer fitted with the paddle attachment, or a large bowl using electric beaters, cream together the butter and sugar on medium speed for about 3 minutes until fluffy, stopping partway through to scrape down the sides of the bowl with a spatula. Turn the mixer to low speed and gradually add the strawberry mixture, a few tablespoons at a time, mixing until well incorporated.

4. Add the dry ingredients. Remove the bowl from the mixer stand. Place a sifter over the bowl. Add the flour, baking powder, and salt to the sifter. Gently shake the sifter to move all the ingredients into the bowl. Using a spatula, gently fold (stir down, over, and up again, repeating in a circle) the flour

mixture into the strawberry mixture until fully incorporated.

5. Fill the pan. Using an ice-cream scoop, divide the batter evenly among the prepared cups, filling each about three-quarters full.

6. Bake. Carefully place the pan onto the center rack of the preheated oven. Bake for 18 to 20 minutes, rotating the pan halfway through baking (use oven mitts!) so your cupcakes bake evenly. The cupcakes are ready when you can press on the top of them with your finger and the cake springs back (ask an adult to help).

7. Let cool. Remove the pan from the oven (use oven mitts!) and place on a wire rack. Let the cupcakes cool in the pan for 10 minutes. Once they're cool enough to touch, remove the cupcakes from the pan and transfer them to the wire rack to cool completely, about 1 hour.

8. Make the frosting. While the cupcakes are cooling, make the fruity buttercream with strawberry jam following the directions on page 129.

9. Frost the cupcakes. Once the cupcakes are completely cooled, frost the cupcakes with a knife, offset spatula, or a piping bag. Add some strawberry slices for a decoration, if desired.

CHOCOLATE CHIP RASPBERRY CUPCAKES

Is there a better combination than chocolate and raspberry? I don't think so! So sweet and light, these cupcakes need only a drizzle of glaze or a sprinkle of powdered sugar to make them sing. If using cupcake liners, choose colorful paper ones to bring even more pizazz to the plate.

| MAKES **12** CUPCAKES | PREP TIME **30** MINUTES | BAKE TIME **20** MINUTES | NUT-FREE |

Super Baker: Frozen raspberries work in this recipe, too! Just toss 1 cup of frozen berries in 2 tablespoons of all-purpose flour before adding to the batter in step 6. The flour helps absorb the extra moisture from the ice around the berries and helps prevent them from sinking.

Change It Up: Make chocolate chip orange cupcakes! Substitute 1 cup of drained and sliced canned orange segments for the raspberries (cut each segment into 3 pieces).

Nonstick cooking spray (optional)
4 tablespoons (½ stick) unsalted butter, at room temperature, plus more for preparing the pan (optional)
⅔ cup sugar
1¼ cups all-purpose flour
1½ teaspoons baking powder
¼ teaspoon fine salt
1 large egg
½ cup whole milk
1 teaspoon pure vanilla extract
½ cup semisweet chocolate chips
1 cup fresh raspberries (see Super Baker tip)

Powdered sugar, for dusting

TOOLS

Standard 12-cup muffin pan
Cupcake liners (optional)
Measuring cups and spoons
Stand mixer fitted with paddle attachment or large bowl and electric beaters
Silicone spatula
Mixing bowls
Whisk or fork
Glass measuring cup
#20 ice-cream scoop with spring release
Oven mitts
Wire rack
Sifter or fine-mesh sieve

1. **Preheat the oven.** Set the oven to 350°F. Line a muffin pan with paper liners, or grease each cup (see page 5).

2. **Cream the butter.** In the bowl of a stand mixer fitted with the paddle attachment, or a large bowl using electric beaters, cream together the butter and sugar on medium speed for about 3 minutes until fluffy, stopping partway through to scrape down the sides of the bowl with a spatula. Once the butter is fluffy, stop the mixer.

3. **Mix the dry ingredients.** In another large bowl, combine the flour, baking powder, and salt. Using a whisk or a fork, stir about 20 times to combine well. Set aside.

4. **Mix the wet ingredients.** Crack the egg into a glass measuring cup with a spout (if you get any shell in it, see page 5 for tips on easily removing it). Add the milk and vanilla. Using a fork, stir until combined. Set aside.

5. **Add the dry ingredients to the wet ingredients.** Pour half the flour mixture into the sugar mixture. Mix on low speed for 10 seconds. Add half the milk mixture. Mix on low speed for 10 seconds more. Stop the mixer and use a spatula to scrape down the sides of the bowl. Add the remaining flour and milk mixtures, mixing for 10 seconds between each addition. Using the spatula, scrape down the sides of the bowl. Stir the batter a few more times just until you can't see any flour.

6. **Add the chocolate and raspberries.** Using a spatula, gently fold (stir down, over, and up again, repeating in a circle) the chocolate chips and raspberries into the batter until fully mixed, about 10 times.

7. **Fill the pan.** Using an ice-cream scoop, divide the batter evenly among the prepared cups, filling each about three-quarters full.

8. **Bake.** Carefully place the pan onto the center rack of the preheated oven. Bake for 18 to 20 minutes, rotating the pan halfway through baking (use oven mitts!) so your cupcakes bake evenly. The cupcakes are ready when you can press on the top of them with your finger and the cake springs back (ask an adult to help).

9. **Let cool.** Remove the pan from the oven (use oven mitts!) and place on a wire rack. Let the cupcakes cool in the pan for 10 minutes. Once they're cool enough to touch, remove the cupcakes from the pan and transfer them to the wire rack to cool completely, about 1 hour.

10. **Garnish.** Just before serving, sprinkle with powdered sugar.

RED VELVET CUPCAKES WITH CREAM CHEESE FROSTING

When it comes to red velvet cake, where did the term "velvet" come from? Back in the 1800s, when cooks started adding cocoa to their flour, they noticed how soft—how velvety—it made the cakes. If you want to achieve that soft, delicate crumb, don't skimp on using the extra bowls for this recipe. Baking is a science and you need to follow the instructions to produce the best results.

Nonstick cooking spray (optional)

6 tablespoons (¾ stick) unsalted butter, at room temperature, plus more for preparing the pan (optional)

½ cup buttermilk (see Super Baker tip)

1½ teaspoons vinegar

2 teaspoons pure vanilla extract

1 large egg

1⅛ cups all-purpose flour

1 tablespoon natural unsweetened cocoa powder (not Dutch-processed)

1 teaspoon baking soda

¼ teaspoon fine salt

¾ cup sugar

5 drops red liquid gel food coloring

1 batch Cream Cheese Frosting (page 131)

TOOLS

Standard 12-cup muffin pan

Cupcake liners (optional)

Measuring cups and spoons

Mixing bowls

Small bowl

Whisk or fork

Stand mixer fitted with paddle attachment or large bowl and electric beaters

Silicone spatula

#20 ice-cream scoop with spring release

Oven mitts

Wire rack

Knife or offset spatula

1. Preheat the oven. Set the oven to 350°F. Line a muffin pan with paper liners, or grease the inside of each cup with cooking spray or butter (see page 5).

2. Mix the wet ingredients. In a large bowl, combine the buttermilk, vinegar, and vanilla. Crack the egg into a small bowl (if you get any shell in it, see page 5 for tips on easily removing it) and add it to the buttermilk mixture. Using a whisk or a fork, mix about 30 times until the egg is fully incorporated. Set aside.

3. Mix the dry ingredients. In another large bowl, combine the flour, cocoa powder, baking soda, and salt. Using a spatula, stir about 10 times. Set aside.

4. Cream the butter. In the bowl of a stand mixer fitted with the paddle attachment, or a large bowl using electric beaters, cream together the butter and sugar on medium speed for about 3 minutes until fluffy, stopping partway through to scrape down the sides of the bowl with a spatula. Once the butter is fluffy, stop the mixer.

5. Add the wet ingredients to the dry ingredients. Add half the flour mixture to the butter mixture. Mix on low speed for 10 seconds until smooth. Add half the buttermilk mixture. Mix on low speed for 10 seconds more. Repeat with the remaining flour and buttermilk mixtures, mixing after each addition until just incorporated. Add the red food coloring and mix on medium-low speed for 5 seconds. Using a spatula, scrape down the sides of the bowl and stir just until the batter looks uniform.

6. Fill the pan. Using an ice-cream scoop, divide the batter evenly among the prepared cups, filling each about three-quarters full.

7. Bake. Carefully place the pan onto the center rack of the preheated oven. Bake for 20 minutes, rotating the pan halfway through baking (use oven mitts!) so your cupcakes bake evenly. The cupcakes are ready when you can press on the top of them with your finger and the cake springs back (ask an adult to help).

8. Let cool. Remove the pan from the oven (use oven mitts!) and place on a wire rack. Let the cupcakes cool in the pan for 10 minutes. Once they're cool enough to touch, remove the cupcakes from the pan and transfer them to the wire rack to cool completely, about 1 hour.

CONTINUED ON NEXT PAGE

9. Make the frosting. While the cupcakes are cooling, make the cream cheese frosting following the directions on page 131.

10. Frost the cupcakes. Once the cupcakes are completely cooled, use a knife or offset spatula to spread an even layer of frosting on top of each cupcake. Add sprinkles for decoration, if desired.

Change It Up: Create a swirl effect by separating your batter into two bowls: add the red food coloring to one bowl and leave the other as is. Pour one scoop of each batter into your cupcake pan and use a toothpick to swirl them together.

Super Baker: No buttermilk? Make your own by adding ½ tablespoon of white vinegar to ½ cup of regular milk. Or use plain yogurt instead.

CHOCOLATE CUPCAKES WITH PEANUT BUTTER FROSTING

These chocolate cupcakes are rich, tangy, and moist, just waiting to be loaded with your favorite frosting: chocolate, vanilla, strawberry, or even peanut butter! This basic recipe can be dolled up with a sprinkle of peppermint candies on top for the holidays, filled with peanut butter, or topped with crushed Oreos to make Oreo Dirt Cups with candy worms, tiny dinosaurs or bulldozers (see page 76). That's only the beginning. It's all up to you!

MAKES	PREP TIME	BAKE TIME
12 CUPCAKES	**25** MINUTES	**20** MINUTES

🏆 **Super Baker:** No buttermilk? Make your own by adding 1 tablespoon of white vinegar to ¾ cup of regular milk and letting it sit for a few minutes. Or substitute an equal amount of plain yogurt.

Nonstick cooking spray (optional)

4 tablespoons (½ stick) unsalted butter, at room temperature, plus more for preparing the pan (optional)

⅔ cup sugar

¾ cup buttermilk (see Super Baker tip)

1 teaspoon pure vanilla extract

1 cup all-purpose flour

⅓ cup unsweetened cocoa powder

1 teaspoon baking soda

½ teaspoon fine salt

1 large egg

1 batch Peanut Butter Frosting (page 132)

TOOLS

Standard 12-cup muffin pan

Cupcake liners (optional)

Measuring cups and spoons

Stand mixer fitted with paddle attachment or large bowl and electric beaters

Silicone spatula

Glass measuring cup

Mixing bowls

Small bowl

#20 ice-cream scoop with spring release

Oven mitts

Wire rack

Knife or offset spatula

CONTINUED ON NEXT PAGE

1. **Preheat the oven.** Set the oven to 350°F. Line a muffin pan with liners, or grease each cup (see page 5).

2. **Cream the butter.** In the bowl of a stand mixer fitted with the paddle attachment, or a large bowl using electric beaters, cream together the butter and sugar on medium speed for about 3 minutes until fluffy, stopping partway through to scrape down the sides of the bowl with a spatula.

3. **Mix the wet ingredients.** In a glass measuring cup with a spout, measure the buttermilk. Add the vanilla, stir, and set aside.

4. **Mix the dry ingredients.** In another large bowl, combine the flour, cocoa powder, baking soda, and salt. Using a spatula, stir about 10 times to combine well. Set aside.

5. **Add the egg.** Crack the egg into a small bowl. Add the egg to the butter mixture. Mix on medium speed for 1 minute.

6. **Add the dry ingredients to the wet ingredients.** Add half the cocoa mixture to the butter mixture. Mix on medium-low speed for 10 seconds just until combined. Add half the buttermilk mixture and mix just for 10 seconds. Add the remaining cocoa and

buttermilk mixtures, mixing for 10 seconds between each addition. Using a spatula, scrape down the sides of the bowl and stir the batter a few more times, just until it comes together.

7. **Fill the pan.** Using an ice-cream scoop, divide the batter evenly among the prepared cups, filling each about three-quarters full.

8. **Bake.** Carefully place the pan onto the center rack of the preheated oven. Bake for 18 to 20 minutes, rotating the pan halfway through baking so your cupcakes bake evenly. They are ready when you can press on the top of them with your finger and the cake springs back (ask an adult to help).

9. **Let cool.** Remove the pan from the oven (use oven mitts!) and place on a wire rack. Let cool in the pan for 10 minutes. Once they're cool enough to touch, remove the cupcakes from the pan and transfer them to the wire rack to cool completely, about 1 hour.

10. **Make the frosting.** Make the peanut butter frosting following the directions on page 132.

11. **Frost the cupcakes.** Use a knife or offset spatula to spread an even layer of frosting on top of each cupcake.

YELLOW CUPCAKES WITH CHOCOLATE BUTTERCREAM

Close your eyes and think of a cupcake. Is it yellow with chocolate frosting on top? That's it! The classic, perfect cupcake gets its color naturally from the butter and egg yolks. My favorite icing to pair with these is chocolate buttercream topped with a pinch of colorful sprinkles.

| MAKES **12** CUPCAKES | PREP TIME **25** MINUTES | BAKE TIME **20** MINUTES | NUT-FREE |

Super Baker: Why didn't we need more bowls? In this case, the extra egg yolks act like delicious glue, bringing the batter together.

Ask an Adult: The only tricky part here is separating the eggs, so ask an adult to help if you need it. See page 5 for handy tips on how to separate eggs.

Nonstick cooking spray (optional)

8 tablespoons (1 stick) unsalted butter, at room temperature, plus more for preparing the pan (optional)

1 cup sugar

1½ cups all-purpose flour

1½ teaspoons baking powder

½ teaspoon fine salt

½ cup full-fat plain yogurt

2 teaspoons pure vanilla extract

3 large eggs, divided

1 batch Chocolate Buttercream (page 135)

TOOLS

Standard 12-cup muffin pan

Cupcake liners (optional)

Measuring cups and spoons

Stand mixer fitted with paddle attachment or large bowl and electric beaters

Silicone spatula

3 small bowls

#20 ice-cream scoop with spring release

Oven mitts

Wire rack

Knife or offset spatula

CONTINUED ON NEXT PAGE

1. **Preheat the oven.** Set the oven to 350°F. Line a muffin pan with paper liners, or grease the inside of each cup with cooking spray or butter (see page 5).

2. **Mix the dry ingredients.** In the bowl of a stand mixer fitted with the paddle attachment, or a large bowl using electric beaters, combine the sugar, flour, baking powder, and salt. Mix on low speed for 30 seconds.

3. **Add the wet ingredients.** Add the butter, yogurt, and vanilla. Mix on medium speed for 30 seconds. Stop the mixer and use the spatula to scrape down the sides of the bowl.

4. **Add the eggs.** Crack 1 egg into a small bowl (if you get any shell in it, see page 5 for tips on easily removing it). Add the egg to your batter. Mix on medium speed for 30 seconds. Separate the remaining 2 eggs (see page 5, or ask an adult to help you) into 2 small bowls (whites in one, yolks in another). Pour just the yolks into the batter (save the whites for another use). Mix on medium speed for about 30 seconds until the batter is silky smooth. Stop the mixer and use the spatula to scrape down the sides of the bowl. Stir the batter a few more times just until you can't see any flour.

5. **Fill the pan.** Using an ice-cream scoop, divide the batter evenly among the prepared cups, filling each about three-quarters full.

6. **Bake.** Carefully place the pan onto the center rack of the preheated oven. Bake for 18 to 20 minutes, rotating the pan halfway through baking (use oven mitts!) so your cupcakes bake evenly. The cupcakes are ready when you can press on the top of them with your finger and the cake springs back (ask an adult to help).

7. **Let cool.** Remove the pan from the oven (use oven mitts!) and place on a wire rack. Let the cupcakes cool in the pan for 10 minutes. Once they're cool enough to touch, remove the cupcakes from the pan and transfer them to the wire rack to cool completely, about 1 hour.

8. **Make the frosting.** While the cupcakes are cooling, make the chocolate buttercream following the directions on page 135.

9. **Frost the cupcakes.** Once the cupcakes are completely cooled, use a knife or offset spatula to spread an even layer of frosting on top of each cupcake.

LEMON CUPCAKES WITH LEMON GLAZE

Sweet and sour all at once, these little lemon cakes are like lemonade on a plate! Want to make them fancy? Turn your cupcakes upside down and serve each one on a delicate dessert plate. Drizzle the glaze over the top and serve them with a fork. Perfect for a tea party or special day with friends.

MAKES	PREP TIME	BAKE TIME	
12 CUPCAKES	**30** MINUTES	**20** MINUTES	NUT-FREE

Change It Up: Make lemon-blueberry cupcakes! You'll need about ¾ cup of fresh blueberries. Lightly dust the blueberries with all-purpose flour (this helps keep the berries from sinking to the bottom of your cupcakes!). In step 6, fill each cup half full with batter, top with a few blueberries, and cover with the remaining batter. Proceed with the recipe as written.

Nonstick cooking spray (optional)

6 tablespoons (¾ stick) unsalted butter, at room temperature, plus more for preparing the pan (optional)

¾ cup sugar

2 teaspoons finely grated lemon zest (from 2 lemons)

1¼ cups all-purpose flour

¾ teaspoon baking powder

½ teaspoon fine salt

1 large egg

¾ cup full-fat sour cream

1 batch Lemon Glaze (page 133)

TOOLS

Standard 12-cup muffin pan

Cupcake liners (optional)

Measuring cups and spoons

Zester or box grater (use the small holes)

Stand mixer fitted with paddle attachment or large bowl and electric beaters

Silicone spatula

Mixing bowls

Whisk or fork

Glass measuring cup

#20 ice-cream scoop with spring release

Oven mitts

Wire rack

Knife or offset spatula

CONTINUED ON NEXT PAGE

1. **Preheat the oven.** Set the oven to 325°F. Line a muffin pan with paper liners, or grease each cup (see page 5).

2. **Cream the butter.** In the bowl of a stand mixer fitted with the paddle attachment, or a large bowl using electric beaters, cream together the butter, sugar, and lemon zest on medium speed for about 3 minutes until fluffy, stopping partway through to scrape down the sides of the bowl with a spatula. Once the butter is fluffy, stop the mixer.

3. **Mix the dry ingredients.** In another large bowl, combine the flour, baking powder, and salt. Stir about 20 times to combine well.

4. **Mix the wet ingredients.** Crack the egg into a glass measuring cup with a spout. Add the sour cream. Using a fork, stir until well combined.

5. **Add the dry ingredients to the wet ingredients.** Pour half the flour mixture into the butter mixture. Mix on low speed for 10 seconds. Add half the sour cream mixture. Mix on low speed for 10 seconds more. Stop the mixer and use the spatula to scrape down the sides of the bowl. Add the remaining flour and sour cream mixtures, mixing for 10 seconds between each addition.

Stir the batter a few more times just until you can't see any flour.

6. **Fill the pan.** Using an ice-cream scoop, divide the batter evenly among the prepared cups, filling each about three-quarters full.

7. **Bake.** Carefully place the pan onto the center rack of the preheated oven. Bake for 18 to 20 minutes, rotating the pan halfway through baking (use oven mitts!). They are ready when you can press on the top of them with your finger and the cake springs back (ask an adult to help).

8. **Let cool.** Remove the pan from the oven (use oven mitts!) and place on a wire rack. Let the cupcakes cool in the pan for 10 minutes. Once they're cool enough to touch, remove the cupcakes from the pan and transfer them to the wire rack to cool completely, about 1 hour.

9. **Make the glaze.** Make the lemon glaze following the directions on page 133.

10. **Glaze the cupcakes.** Once the cupcakes are completely cooled, drizzle the glaze on top of each cupcake. Or turn the cupcakes upside down and serve on a dessert plate—like a mini cake—then drizzle with lemon glaze.

CARROT CAKE CUPCAKES WITH CREAM CHEESE FROSTING

Some historians believe that people have been baking carrot cakes since the Middle Ages when sugar was so expensive only the very rich could afford it. With lots of natural sweetness, carrots became a substitute for sugar. These days sugar is easier to afford, but one fact remains true: No cupcake is ever as moist as carrot cake! Slathered with cream cheese frosting, it's no wonder carrot cake has been a favorite for hundreds of years.

MAKES	PREP TIME	BAKE TIME	
12 CUPCAKES	**25** MINUTES	**20** MINUTES	NUT-FREE

 **Change It Up:** Substitute an equal amount of crushed pineapple for the grated carrots. Or, for a crunchy protein boost, add ½ cup of chopped walnuts, if you can eat nuts.

Nonstick cooking spray, or unsalted butter for preparing the pan (optional)

2 large carrots

2 large eggs

½ cup vegetable oil

1 cup all-purpose flour

¾ cup sugar

1 teaspoon ground cinnamon

1 teaspoon baking powder

½ teaspoon fine salt

1 batch Cream Cheese Frosting (page 131)

TOOLS

Standard 12-cup muffin pan

Cupcake liners (optional)

Box grater

Cutting board

Measuring cups and spoons

Stand mixer fitted with paddle attachment or large bowl and electric beaters

Small bowl

Silicone spatula

Sifter

#20 ice-cream scoop with spring release

Oven mitts

Wire rack

Knife or offset spatula

CONTINUED ON NEXT PAGE

CARROT CAKE CUPCAKES WITH CREAM CHEESE FROSTING

CONTINUED

1. **Preheat the oven.** Set the oven to 350°F. Line a muffin pan with paper liners, or grease the inside of each cup with cooking spray or butter (see page 5).

2. **Grate the carrots.** No need to peel your carrots; just wash them carefully. Using the large holes on a box grater, grate the carrots over a cutting board (watch your knuckles!). Transfer the grated carrots to the bowl of the stand mixer fitted with the paddle attachment, or a large bowl using electric beaters.

3. **Add the wet ingredients.** Crack 1 egg into a small bowl (if you get any shell in it, see page 5 for tips on easily removing it), then add it to the carrots. Repeat with the remaining egg. Add the oil. Mix for 2 minutes until fluffy. Stop the mixer and use a spatula to scrape down the sides of the bowl.

4. **Add the dry ingredients.** Remove the bowl from the mixer stand. Place a sifter over the bowl. Add the flour, sugar, cinnamon, baking powder, and salt to the sifter. Gently shake the sifter to move all the ingredients into the bowl. Using a spatula, gently fold (stir down, over, and up again, repeating in a circle) the flour mixture into the carrot mixture until fully incorporated.

5. **Fill the pan.** Using an ice-cream scoop, divide the batter evenly among the prepared cups, filling each about three-quarters full.

6. **Bake.** Carefully place the pan onto the center rack of the preheated oven. Bake for 18 to 20 minutes, rotating the pan halfway through baking (use oven mitts!) so your cupcakes bake evenly. The cupcakes are ready when you can press on the top of them with your finger and the cake springs back (ask an adult to help).

7. **Let cool.** Remove the pan from the oven (use oven mitts!) and place on a wire rack. Let the cupcakes cool in the pan for 10 minutes. Once they're cool enough to touch, remove the cupcakes from the pan and transfer them to the wire rack to cool completely, about 1 hour.

8. **Make the frosting.** While the cupcakes are cooling, make the cream cheese frosting following the directions on page 131.

9. **Frost the cupcakes.** Once the cupcakes are completely cooled, use a knife or offset spatula to spread an even layer of frosting on top of each cupcake.

VANILLA CUPCAKES WITH S'MORES ON TOP

There's nothing simpler than a perfect vanilla cupcake. And the options for changing it up are endless! To the batter, add crushed Oreos for Cookies & Cream cupcakes (page 76). Stir in a cup of sprinkles for birthday cake cupcakes. Crush your favorite chocolates to make candy bar cupcakes. On and on, you get to decide, starting with one easy recipe. Speaking of sweets, try topping these with s'mores! Get the ooey-gooey details for this surprisingly simple technique on page 137, no campfire required.

MAKES	PREP TIME	BAKE TIME	NUT-FREE
12 CUPCAKES	**30** MINUTES	**20** MINUTES	

Nonstick cooking spray (optional)

8 tablespoons (1 stick) unsalted butter, at room temperature, plus more for preparing the pan (optional)

1 cup sugar

1½ cups all-purpose flour

1½ teaspoons baking powder

½ teaspoon fine salt

½ cup whole milk

2 teaspoons pure vanilla extract

2 large eggs

1 batch S'mores on Top (page 137)

TOOLS

Standard 12-cup muffin pan

Cupcake liners (optional)

Measuring cups and spoons

Stand mixer fitted with paddle attachment or large bowl and electric beaters

Silicone spatula

Mixing bowls

Whisk or fork

Glass measuring cup

Small bowl

#20 ice-cream scoop with spring release

Oven mitts

Wire rack

Knife or offset spatula

CONTINUED ON NEXT PAGE

1. **Preheat the oven.** Set the oven to 350°F. Line a muffin pan with paper liners, or grease the inside of each cup with cooking spray or butter (see page 5).

2. **Cream the butter.** In the bowl of a stand mixer fitted with the paddle attachment, or a large bowl using electric beaters, cream together the butter and sugar on medium speed for about 3 minutes until fluffy, stopping partway through to scrape down the sides of the bowl with a spatula. Once the butter is fluffy, stop the mixer.

3. **Mix the dry ingredients.** In another large bowl, combine the flour, baking powder, and salt. Using a whisk or fork, stir about 20 times, until well incorporated.

4. **Mix the wet ingredients.** In a glass measuring cup, measure the milk and add the vanilla. Stir well and set aside.

5. **Add the eggs.** Crack 1 egg into a small bowl (if you get any shell in it, see page 5 for tips on easily removing it). Add the egg to the butter mixture. Mix on medium speed for 1 minute. Stop the mixer and use the spatula to scrape down the sides of the bowl. Add the second egg. Mix for 1 minute. Stop and scrape down the bowl again.

6. **Add the dry ingredients to the wet ingredients.** Pour half the flour mixture into the butter and egg mixture. Mix on low speed for 10 seconds. Add half the milk mixture. Mix on low speed for 10 seconds more. Stop the mixer and use the spatula to scrape down the sides of the bowl. Add the remaining flour and milk mixtures, mixing for 10 seconds between each addition. Using the spatula, scrape down the sides of the bowl. Stir the batter a few more times just until you can't see any flour.

7. **Fill the pan.** Using an ice-cream scoop, divide the batter evenly among the prepared cups, filling each about three-quarters full.

8. **Bake.** Carefully place the pan onto the center rack of the preheated oven. Bake for 18 to 20 minutes, rotating the pan halfway through baking (use oven mitts!) so your cupcakes bake evenly. The cupcakes are ready when you can press on the top of them with your finger and the cake springs back (ask an adult to help).

9. **Let cool.** Remove the pan from the oven (use oven mitts!) and place on a wire rack. Let the cupcakes cool in the pan for 10 minutes. Once they're cool

enough to touch, remove the cupcakes from the pan and transfer them to the wire rack to cool completely, about 1 hour.

10. **Add the topping.** Add s'mores on top following the directions on page 137.

Decorating Tip: One of my favorite ways to decorate vanilla cupcakes is using Vanilla Buttercream (page 128), then adding 2 or 3 pieces of fresh fruit and a tiny mint sprig on top. The color combination is unbeatable. Just decorate the cupcakes right before serving so the icing doesn't get soggy.

chapter 3
FUN-FILLED CUPCAKES

With a surprise in every bite,
these treats pack an extra punch of
flavor on the inside!

Need more photos? Visit my website at Foodlets.com/cupcakes for pictures of each recipe.

CHOCOLATE-HAZELNUT CUPCAKES INSIDE AND OUT

We made these cupcakes for my daughter's ninth birthday, and it was extra sweet because both the birthday girl and Nutella (the brand we used) were born in Italy. Did you know this sweet and nutty spread was originally developed because of a chocolate shortage? After World War II, it was difficult to find cocoa. So, an Italian pastry maker developed this gorgeously gooey paste using hazelnuts and sugar with just a *pinch* of cocoa. Now it's enjoyed in countries all over the world, in your kitchen and mine, too.

MAKES **12** CUPCAKES

PREP TIME **40** MINUTES

BAKE TIME **20** MINUTES

Nonstick cooking spray (optional)

8 tablespoons (1 stick) unsalted butter, at room temperature, plus more for preparing the pan (optional)

1 cup all-purpose flour

½ cup unsweetened cocoa powder

½ teaspoon baking powder

½ teaspoon baking soda

¾ cup sugar

¾ cup chocolate-hazelnut spread (such as Nutella), divided

1 teaspoon pure vanilla extract

2 large eggs

½ cup buttermilk

1 batch Chocolate-Hazelnut Frosting (page 136)

TOOLS

Standard 12-cup muffin pan

Cupcake liners (optional)

Measuring cups and spoons

Mixing bowls

Whisk

Stand mixer fitted with paddle attachment or large bowl and electric beaters

Small bowl

Silicone spatula

#20 ice-cream scoop with spring release

Oven mitts

Wire rack

Paring knife
Spoon

1. **Preheat the oven.** Set the oven to 350°F. Line a muffin pan with paper liners, or grease the inside of each cup with cooking spray or butter (see page 5).

2. **Prepare the dry ingredients.** In a medium bowl, whisk the flour, cocoa powder, baking powder, and baking soda until completely combined.

3. **Cream the butter.** In the bowl of a stand mixer fitted with the paddle attachment, or large bowl using electric beaters, cream together the butter, sugar, ¼ cup of chocolate-hazelnut spread, and vanilla on medium speed for about 3 minutes until smooth.

4. **Add the eggs.** Crack 1 egg into a small bowl (if you get any shell in it, see page 5 for tips on easily removing it). Pour the egg into the butter mixture. Mix for 1 minute. Stop the mixer and use a spatula to scrape down the sides of the bowl. Repeat with the remaining egg. Mix again for 1 minute.

5. **Combine the flour mixture.** Turn the mixer on low speed and slowly add half the flour mixture. Add half the buttermilk. Repeat until all flour and buttermilk are in the mixture. Stop the mixer when the flour is just combined. Using a silicone spatula, scrape down the sides of the bowl.

6. **Fill the pan.** Using an ice-cream scoop, divide the batter evenly among the prepared cups, filling each about three-quarters full.

7. **Bake.** Carefully place the pan onto the center rack of the preheated oven. Bake for 18 to 20 minutes, rotating the pan halfway through baking (use oven mitts!) so your cupcakes bake evenly. The cupcakes are ready when you can press on the top of them with your finger and the cake springs back (ask an adult to help).

8. **Let cool.** Remove the pan from the oven (use oven mitts!) and place on a wire rack. Let the cupcakes cool in the pan for 10 minutes. Once they're cool enough to touch, remove the cupcakes from the pan and transfer them to the wire rack to cool completely, about 1 hour.

9. **Make the frosting.** While the cupcakes are cooling, make the chocolate-hazelnut frosting following the directions on page 136.

10. **Assemble the cupcakes.** After the cupcakes have cooled completely, ask an adult to help you cut a cone shape out of the top of each cupcake. Trim off the bottom (pointy) part of the cones. Use a tiny spoon to place a dollop of the remaining ½ cup chocolate-hazelnut spread inside the hole and place the tops back on.

CONTINUED ON NEXT PAGE

11. Frost the cupcakes. Once the cupcakes are filled, use a spoon to dollop the frosting on top of each cupcake.

Decorating Tip: These cupcakes look beautiful with a big dollop of chocolate-hazelnut frosting. To make the edges neat, fill a pastry bag fitted with an extra-large tip, or a resealable bag with a corner tip snipped off, to squeeze out the frosting like you're filling a soft-serve ice-cream cone. Place a golden-covered chocolate on top, and you've got an Italian delicacy in your hand.

BLACK-BOTTOM CUPCAKES

What's a "black bottom?" That's the chocolate part of these cupcakes—and it's only the beginning. These beauties have a tiny cheesecake baked right on top. And if that wasn't enough, you'll add a luscious sprinkle of chocolate chips. Don't adjust your eyes, though, because you won't find any eggs in the ingredients for these cupcakes. Instead, you'll use the combination of balsamic vinegar and baking soda to produce enough air to make them rise! Both parts of the batter will seem runny, so just have faith. Once they bake, everything firms right up. I loved these cupcakes as a kid when my mom used to make them, and now I'm so excited to share the recipe with you.

MAKES 12 CUPCAKES

MAKES 1½ CUPS FILLING

PREP TIME 40 MINUTES

BAKE TIME 25 MINUTES

NUT-FREE

FOR THE CUPCAKES

Nonstick cooking spray, or unsalted butter for preparing the pan (optional)
½ cup cold water
¼ cup vegetable oil
1½ teaspoons balsamic vinegar
1 teaspoon pure vanilla extract
1 cup all-purpose flour
½ cup sugar
¼ cup unsweetened cocoa powder
½ teaspoon baking soda
¼ teaspoon fine salt
¼ cup semisweet chocolate chips

FOR THE FILLING

4 ounces (½ block) full-fat cream cheese, at room temperature
¼ cup sugar
1 large egg

TOOLS

Measuring cups and spoons
Stand mixer fitted with paddle attachment or large bowl and electric beaters
Small bowl
Silicone spatula
Standard 12-cup muffin pan
Cupcake liners (optional)
Mixing bowls
Sifter
#20 ice-cream scoop with spring release
Spoon

CONTINUED ON NEXT PAGE

Wooden skewer

Wire rack

TO MAKE THE FILLING

1. Prepare the filling. In the bowl of a stand mixer fitted with the paddle attachment, or a large bowl using electric beaters, combine the cream cheese and sugar. Crack the egg into a small bowl (if you get any shell in it, see page 5 for tips on easily removing it) and add it to the bowl. Mix on medium speed for about 2 minutes. Stop the mixer and use a spatula to scrape down the sides of the bowl. Mix for 10 seconds more. Set aside.

TO MAKE THE CUPCAKES

2. Preheat the oven. Set the oven to 350°F. Line a muffin pan with paper liners, or grease the inside of each cup with cooking spray or butter (see page 5).

3. Prepare the batter. In a large bowl, combine the cold water, oil, vinegar, and vanilla. Place a sifter over the top of the bowl and add the flour, sugar, cocoa powder, baking soda, and salt to the sifter. Gently shake the sifter to move all the ingredients into the bowl. Using a spatula, stir until the batter is smooth. (Don't worry, it'll be runny and a bit lumpy!)

4. Fill the pan. Using an ice-cream scoop, divide the batter evenly among the prepared cups, filling each about three-quarters full. Using a spoon, place about 2 tablespoons of cream cheese filling in the center of each cupcake, letting it sink down a bit. Sprinkle 7 or 8 chocolate chips on top of each.

5. Bake. Carefully place the pan onto the center rack of the preheated oven. Bake for 23 to 25 minutes, or until the centers of the cupcakes are set and the edges look firm (poke a cupcake with a wooden skewer or toothpick; if it comes out clean, the cupcakes are ready).

6. Let cool. Remove the pan from the oven (use oven mitts!) and place on a wire rack. Let the cupcakes cool in the pan for 10 minutes. Once they're cool enough to touch, remove the cupcakes from the pan and transfer them to the wire rack to cool completely, about 1 hour.

🏆 **Super Baker:** Always put your pan on the center rack of the oven. Most ovens have hot spots (and cooler areas, too). Your best bet for cooking evenly, as close to the time and temperature in the recipe, is baking right in the center of the oven.

BOSTON CREAM CUPCAKES WITH CHOCOLATE GLAZE

I made these for a dinner party with neighbors who didn't stop talking about them . . . for a year! The combination of spongy yellow cake with a thick layer of vanilla cream topped with a simple chocolate glaze? It's unbeatable. And instead of cutting out the center of these cupcakes, you slice the whole cupcake apart from the side, making a perfect miniature version of Boston cream pie, only this kind fits in your hand.

MAKES **12** CUPCAKES

MAKES **2** CUPS FILLING

PREP TIME **40** MINUTES

BAKE TIME **20** MINUTES

NUT-FREE

FOR THE CUPCAKES

Nonstick cooking spray (optional)

12 tablespoons (1½ sticks) unsalted butter, cut into 12 pieces, at room temperature, plus more for preparing the pan (optional)

1¾ cups all-purpose flour, plus more for preparing the pan

1 cup sugar

1½ teaspoons baking powder

¾ teaspoon fine salt

2 large eggs

¾ cup whole milk

1½ teaspoons pure vanilla extract

1 batch Chocolate Glaze (page 134)

FOR THE FILLING

1 (3.4-ounce) package instant vanilla pudding

2 cups heavy (whipping) cream

TOOLS

Standard 12-cup muffin pan

Measuring cups and spoons

Stand mixer fitted with paddle attachment and whisk attachment or large bowl and electric beaters

Small bowl

Silicone spatula

CONTINUED ON NEXT PAGE

#20 ice-cream scoop with
spring release

Oven mitts

Wire rack

Bread knife

Spoon

TO MAKE THE CUPCAKES AND GLAZE

1. **Preheat the oven.** Set the oven to 350°F. Grease the inside of each cup with cooking spray or butter (see page 5), then sprinkle flour inside each cup and shake out any excess.

2. **Prepare the dry ingredients.** In the bowl of the stand mixer fitted with the paddle attachment, or a large bowl using electric beaters, combine the flour, sugar, baking powder, and salt. Mix on low speed for about 20 seconds, just to combine.

3. **Add the butter.** One piece at a time, add the butter and mix on medium speed just until the mixture resembles sand.

4. **Add the eggs.** Crack 1 egg into a small bowl (if you get any shell in it, see page 5 for tips on easily removing it). Add the egg to the flour mixture. Mix on medium speed for 1 minute. Stop the mixer and use a spatula to scrape down the sides of the bowl. Repeat with the remaining egg, mixing for 1 minute.

5. **Add the wet ingredients.** Pour the milk and vanilla into the batter. Mix on medium speed for about 2 minutes until light and fluffy.

6. **Fill the pan.** Using an ice-cream scoop, divide the batter evenly among the prepared cups, filling each about three-quarters full.

7. **Bake.** Carefully place the pan onto the center rack of the preheated oven. Bake for 18 to 20 minutes, rotating the pan halfway through baking (use oven mitts!) so your cupcakes bake evenly. The cupcakes are ready when you can press on the top of them with your finger and the cake springs back (ask an adult to help).

8. **Let cool.** Remove the pan from the oven (use oven mitts!) and place on a wire rack. Let the cupcakes cool in the pan for 10 minutes. Once they're cool enough to touch, remove the cupcakes from the pan and transfer them to the wire rack to cool completely, about 1 hour.

9. **Make the glaze.** While the cupcakes are cooling, make the chocolate glaze following the directions on page 134.

TO MAKE THE FILLING

10. **Make the filling.** Rinse out the bowl for the stand mixer or beaters. Combine the pudding and heavy cream in the bowl. Using the whisk attachment, or electric beaters, beat for about 2 minutes until fluffy (the mixture should be firm enough to stay on the whisk). Put the vanilla cream in the refrigerator while the cupcakes cool.

11. **Assemble the cupcakes.** Ask an adult to help you cut each cupcake in half horizontally with a knife (to separate the bottom from the top). Using a spoon, spread a thick layer of vanilla cream filling on the bottom half of each cupcake. Cover with the top half (like making a sandwich).

12. **Glaze the cupcakes.** Using a clean spoon, spread chocolate glaze over the top of each cupcake.

Change It Up: Instead of going with chocolate glaze, top these with Vanilla Buttercream (page 128) and then sprinkle with fresh berries. Go all red (strawberries and raspberries) for Valentine's Day or red and blue (raspberries and blueberries) for the Fourth of July. Just be sure to add the fruit right before serving or your frosting may get soggy.

COOKIE DOUGH-FILLED VANILLA CUPCAKES WITH CHOCOLATE BUTTERCREAM

Do you love cookie dough as much as I do? Don't worry, this filling is safe to eat raw, with all the flavor of your favorite recipe. I love this combination for Colorful Cookie Monsters (page 93) with adorable blue piping and big candy eyes. Or just add a cute mini chocolate chip cookie to the top of your frosting. A garnish is always a fun way to hint at the special cookie surprise inside!

MAKES 12 CUPCAKES

MAKES 1 CUP FILLING

PREP TIME 40 MINUTES

BAKE TIME 20 MINUTES

NUT-FREE

FOR THE CUPCAKES

Nonstick cooking spray (optional)

8 tablespoons (1 stick) unsalted butter, at room temperature, plus more for preparing the pan (optional)

1⅓ cups all-purpose flour

1 teaspoon baking powder

½ teaspoon fine salt

1 cup sugar

2 large eggs

½ cup whole milk

2 teaspoons pure vanilla extract

½ cup mini chocolate chips

1 batch Chocolate Buttercream (page 135)

FOR THE FILLING

4 tablespoons (½ stick) unsalted butter, at room temperature

⅓ cup packed light brown sugar

½ cup all-purpose flour

⅛ teaspoon fine salt

TOOLS

Standard 12-cup muffin pan

Cupcake liners (optional)

Mixing bowls

Measuring cups and spoons

Whisk

Stand mixer fitted with paddle attachment or large bowl and electric beaters

Silicone spatula

Small bowl

Glass measuring cup

#20 ice-cream scoop with spring release

Oven mitts

Wire rack

Paring knife

Spoon

Knife or offset spatula

TO MAKE THE CUPCAKES AND FROSTING

1. **Preheat the oven.** Set the oven to 350°F. Line a muffin pan with paper liners, or grease the inside of each cup with cooking spray or butter (see page 5).

2. **Prepare the dry ingredients.** In a large bowl, whisk the flour, baking powder, and salt to combine. Set aside.

3. **Cream the butter.** In the bowl of a stand mixer with the paddle attachment, or a large bowl using electric beaters, cream together the butter and sugar on medium-high speed for about 3 minutes until fluffy. Stop the mixer and use a silicone spatula to scrape down the sides of the bowl.

4. **Add the eggs.** Crack 1 egg into a small bowl (if you get any shell in it, see page 5 for tips on easily removing it). Add the egg to the butter mixture. Mix on medium speed for 1 minute. Stop the mixer and use a spatula to scrape down the sides of the bowl. Repeat with the remaining egg, mixing for 1 minute more.

5. **Mix the wet ingredients.** Pour the milk into a glass measuring cup with a spout. Add the vanilla and stir well.

6. **Combine the wet ingredients and the dry ingredients.** Turn the mixer on low speed. Add half the flour mixture to the butter mixture and beat for 10 seconds until you can't see flour anymore. Add half the milk mixture and beat for 10 seconds more. Repeat until all the ingredients are together in the bowl, stopping when just combined. Do not overmix!

7. **Stir in the chocolate chips.** Using a spatula, fold (stir down, over, and up again, repeating in a circle) in the chocolate chips.

8. **Fill the pan.** Using an ice-cream scoop, divide the batter evenly among the prepared cups, filling each about three-quarters full.

9. **Bake.** Carefully place the pan onto the center rack of the preheated oven. Bake for 18 to 20 minutes, rotating the pan halfway through baking (use oven mitts!) so your cupcakes bake evenly. The cupcakes are ready when you can press on the top of them with your

CONTINUED ON NEXT PAGE

finger and the cake springs back (ask an adult to help).

10. **Let cool.** Remove the pan from the oven (use oven mitts!) and place on a wire rack. Let the cupcakes cool in the pan for 10 minutes. Once they're cool enough to touch, remove the cupcakes from the pan and transfer them to the wire rack to cool completely, about 1 hour.

11. **Make the frosting.** While the cupcakes are cooling, make the chocolate buttercream following the directions on page 135.

TO MAKE THE FILLING

12. **Make the cookie dough filling.** While the cupcakes are cooling, wash out the bowl for the stand mixer or beaters and combine the butter and brown sugar in it. Using the paddle attachment or electric beaters, beat on medium speed for about 2 minutes until fluffy. Turn the mixer to low and add

1 tablespoon of water, the flour, and salt. Mix until just combined.

13. **Assemble the cupcakes.** After the cupcakes have cooled completely, ask an adult to help you cut a cone shape out of the top of each cupcake. Trim off the bottom (pointy) part of the cone. Using a tiny spoon, place a dollop of the filling inside the hole and place the tops back on.

14. **Frost the cupcakes.** Once the cupcakes are completely cooled, use a knife or offset spatula to spread an even layer of frosting on top of each cupcake.

🏆 Super Baker: Let's talk storage. Plain cupcakes can be stored on a counter in an airtight container for a couple of days. But once you add filling and frosting, it's better to keep them in the refrigerator. You can also freeze plain cupcakes for weeks in a resealable bag. Just let the cupcakes come to room temperature before frosting.

BANANA CREAM CUPCAKES

We live in the South, where banana pudding is served in almost every restaurant and everyone's grandma has a killer recipe. Now you have one, too—in cupcake form! This sweet treat gets its flavor from real bananas. Ask an adult to help separate an egg for the batter. That extra yolk helps your cupcakes hold more moisture plus makes the crumb strong enough to hold up to the filling inside and a heap of frosting on top. I like to serve these cupcakes with Vanilla or Chocolate Buttercream (page 128 or 135) and a banana chip.

MAKES **12** CUPCAKES

MAKES **1** CUP FILLING

PREP TIME **40** MINUTES

BAKE TIME **20** MINUTES

NUT-FREE

FOR THE CUPCAKES

Nonstick cooking spray (optional)

4 tablespoons (½ stick) unsalted butter, at room temperature, plus more for preparing the pan (optional)

1½ cups all-purpose flour

½ teaspoon baking soda

½ teaspoon baking powder

½ teaspoon ground cinnamon

¼ teaspoon fine salt

2 very ripe bananas

½ cup packed light brown sugar

2 large eggs

1 teaspoon pure vanilla extract

½ cup buttermilk

1 batch Chocolate Buttercream (page 135) or Vanilla Buttercream (page 128)

Banana chips, for garnish (optional)

FOR THE FILLING

1 ripe banana (the browner the better!)

¼ cup plain yogurt

¼ cup heavy (whipping) cream

1 tablespoon powdered sugar

TOOLS

Standard 12-cup muffin pan

Cupcake liners (optional)

Measuring cups and spoons

Mixing bowls

Whisk

CONTINUED ON NEXT PAGE

BANANA CREAM CUPCAKES

CONTINUED

Stand mixer fitted with paddle
attachment or large bowl and
electric beaters

2 small bowls

Silicone spatula

#20 ice-cream scoop with
spring release

Oven mitts

Wire rack

Paring knife

Spoon

Knife or offset spatula

TO MAKE THE CUPCAKES AND FROSTING

1. Preheat the oven. Set the oven
to 350°F. Line a muffin pan with paper
liners, or grease the inside of each
cup with cooking spray or butter
(see page 5).

2. Prepare the dry ingredients. In a
medium bowl, whisk the flour, baking
soda, baking powder, cinnamon, and
salt to combine.

3. Cream the banana and butter. In
the bowl of a stand mixer fitted with the
paddle attachment, or a large bowl
using electric beaters, cream together
the bananas, butter, and brown sugar
on medium speed for about 1 minute
until smooth.

4. Add the eggs and vanilla. Crack
1 egg into a small bowl (if you get any
shell in it, see page 5 for tips on easily
removing it). Add the egg to the banana
mixture. Mix on medium speed for
1 minute. Separate the remaining egg
(see page 5, or ask an adult to help you)
into 2 small bowls (white in one, yolk in
another). Pour just the yolk into the
banana mixture (save the white for
another use). Beat for 1 minute more.
Use a silicone spatula to scrape down
the sides of the bowl. Add the vanilla
and beat for 30 seconds.

5. Combine the ingredients. Add half
the flour mixture to the bowl and turn
the mixer to low speed. With the mixer
running, add half the buttermilk. Repeat
until the flour mixture and buttermilk
are combined with the other ingredients. Do not overmix!

6. Fill the pan. Using an ice-cream
scoop, divide the batter evenly among
the prepared cups, filling each about
three-quarters full.

7. Bake. Carefully place the pan onto
the center rack of the preheated oven.
Bake for 18 to 20 minutes, rotating the
pan halfway through baking (use oven
mitts!) so your cupcakes bake evenly.
The cupcakes are ready when you can

press on the top of them with your finger and the cake springs back (ask an adult to help).

8. **Let cool.** Remove the pan from the oven (use oven mitts!) and place on a wire rack. Let the cupcakes cool in the pan for 10 minutes. Once they're cool enough to touch, remove the cupcakes from the pan and transfer them to the wire rack to cool completely, about 1 hour.

9. **Make the frosting.** While the cupcakes are cooling, make the chocolate buttercream or vanilla buttercream following the directions on page 135 or page 128.

TO MAKE THE FILLING

10. **Make the banana filling.** Wash the bowl and paddle attachment or beaters. Place the banana in the bowl and beat on medium speed for about 30 seconds until smooth. Add the yogurt, heavy cream, and powdered sugar. Beat on medium-high speed for about 2 minutes until stiff peaks form. Refrigerate the filling while the cupcakes cool.

11. **Assemble the cupcakes.** After the cupcakes have cooled completely, ask an adult to help you cut a cone shape out of the top of each cupcake. Trim off the bottom (pointy) part of the cones. Use a tiny spoon to place a dollop of banana filling inside the hole and place the tops back on.

12. **Frost the cupcakes.** Once the cupcakes are filled, use a knife or offset spatula to spread an even layer of frosting on top of each cupcake. Top with a crispy banana chip, if you like.

Super Baker: This recipe only works with very ripe bananas. Why? The longer bananas have to ripen, the more their starch turns to sugar. Greenish bananas might be a better snack to throw in your backpack, but they don't add enough sweetness to be used in cupcakes.

CINNAMON SPICE CUPCAKES WITH APPLE PIE FILLING

Start with this spice cake recipe and you'll have the base for a TON of yummy treats. (Read the Change It Up tip at the end of the recipe for ideas.) Don't worry if you don't have all the spices called for. If you're out of nutmeg, just add a little extra ginger. Ditto for cinnamon and so on. Or, instead of using all three spices individually (cinnamon, nutmeg, and ginger) substitute 1 teaspoon of pumpkin pie spice.

| MAKES **12** CUPCAKES | MAKES **1** CUP FILLING | PREP TIME **40** MINUTES | BAKE TIME **20** MINUTES |

NUT-FREE

FOR THE CUPCAKES

Nonstick cooking spray (optional)

8 tablespoons (1 stick) unsalted butter, melted, plus more for preparing the pan (optional)

1¼ cups all-purpose flour

½ teaspoon baking powder

½ teaspoon baking soda

½ teaspoon fine salt

½ teaspoon ground cinnamon

¼ teaspoon ground nutmeg

¼ teaspoon ground ginger

1 cup packed light brown sugar

½ cup full-fat sour cream

1 teaspoon pure vanilla extract

2 large eggs

1 batch Vanilla Buttercream (page 128) or Cream Cheese Frosting (page 131)

FOR THE FILLING

2 apples (Granny Smith is my favorite)

1 tablespoon unsalted butter, at room temperature

½ teaspoon ground cinnamon

¼ cup sugar

5 tablespoons of water, divided

1 tablespoon cornstarch

TOOLS

Standard 12-cup muffin pan

Cupcake liners (optional)

Measuring cups and spoons

Mixing bowls

Whisk

Stand mixer fitted with paddle attachment or large bowl and electric beaters

Small bowl

Silicone spatula

#20 ice-cream scoop with spring release

Oven mitts

Wire rack

Paring knife

Medium saucepan

Spoon

Knife or offset spatula

TO MAKE THE CUPCAKES AND FROSTING

1. Preheat the oven. Set the oven to 350°F. Line a muffin pan with paper liners, or grease the inside of each cup with cooking spray or butter (see page 5).

2. Prepare the dry ingredients. In a medium bowl, whisk the flour, baking powder, baking soda, salt, cinnamon, nutmeg, and ginger until completely combined.

3. Cream the butter. In the bowl of a stand mixer fitted with the paddle attachment, or a large bowl using electric beaters, cream together the melted butter, brown sugar, sour cream, and vanilla on medium speed until smooth.

4. Add the eggs. Crack 1 egg into a small bowl (if you get any shell in it, see page 5 for tips on easily removing it). Add the egg to the butter mixture. Mix on medium speed for 30 seconds. Stop the mixer and use a spatula to scrape down the sides of the bowl. Repeat with the remaining egg. Beat for 30 seconds more.

5. Combine the flour mixture. Turn the mixer on low speed and slowly add the flour mixture. Stop the mixer when the flour mixture is just combined.

6. Fill the pan. Using an ice-cream scoop, divide the batter evenly among the prepared cups, filling each about three-quarters full.

7. Bake. Carefully place the pan onto the center rack of the preheated oven. Bake for 18 to 20 minutes, rotating the pan halfway through baking (use oven mitts!) so your cupcakes bake evenly. The cupcakes are ready when you can press on the top of them with your finger and the cake springs back (ask an adult to help).

8. Let cool. Remove the pan from the oven (use oven mitts!) and place on a wire rack. Let the cupcakes cool in the pan for 10 minutes. Once they're cool enough to touch, remove the cupcakes from the pan and transfer them to the wire rack to cool completely, about 1 hour.

CONTINUED ON NEXT PAGE

9. Make the frosting. While the cupcakes are cooling, make the vanilla buttercream or cream cheese frosting following the directions on page 128 or page 131.

TO MAKE THE FILLING

10. Make the apple pie filling. Ask an adult to help peel, core, and chop the apples. In a medium saucepan over medium heat, melt the butter and cinnamon. Add the apples, sugar, and 3 tablespoons of water. Cook for 4 to 6 minutes until the apples soften. In a small bowl, stir together the cornstarch and 2 tablespoons of water, stirring until the cornstarch dissolves. Pour the cornstarch mixture into the apples and stir. Let bubble for 1 minute. Set aside to cool.

11. Assemble the cupcakes. After the cupcakes have cooled completely, ask an adult to help you cut a cone shape out of the top of each cupcake. Trim off the bottom (pointy) part of the cones. Use a tiny spoon to place a dollop of the apple pie filling inside the hole and place the tops back on.

12. Frost the cupcakes. Once the cupcakes are filled, use a knife or offset spatula to spread an even layer of frosting on top of each cupcake.

Change It Up: Fill with the apple pie filling as described here or skip the apples altogether. Instead, use walnuts and cranberries for a festive holiday dessert, topped with Vanilla Buttercream (page 128). For a fun Mother's Day tea, turn these cupcakes into individual coffee cakes with a crumble topping: Mix 1 cup of packed light brown sugar with 2 teaspoons of cinnamon, 1 cup of melted butter, and 2½ cups of all-purpose flour. Add a generous amount to the top of each cupcake before baking and add 5 minutes to the baking time. You'll have the perfect dessert to go with any kind of coffee or tea.

CREAMY DREAMY ORANGE CUPCAKES WITH FRUITY BUTTERCREAM

Have you ever had a creamy orange-vanilla ice-cream bar on a hot summer day? There's something magical about the combination of tart orange with smooth vanilla, and these cupcakes capture both beautifully—for every season! This is a three-bowl recipe, and even though you'll have more dishes to clean, don't be tempted to cut corners. Alternating wet and dry ingredients at the end is exactly what makes these cupcakes light and fluffy. Tip: Zest the oranges before cutting them to get the juice out.

MAKES **12** CUPCAKES	MAKES **1** CUP FILLING	PREP TIME **40** MINUTES	BAKE TIME **18** MINUTES
NUT-FREE			

FOR THE CUPCAKES

Nonstick cooking spray (optional)

8 tablespoons (1 stick) unsalted butter, at room temperature, plus more for preparing the pan (optional)

½ cup buttermilk, or plain full-fat yogurt

Juice of 1 orange

1 teaspoon pure vanilla extract

1¾ cups all-purpose flour

1 teaspoon baking powder

½ teaspoon baking soda

½ teaspoon fine salt

1 cup sugar

Zest of 3 oranges

¼ cup orange marmalade

3 large eggs

1 batch Fruity Buttercream (page 129)

FOR THE FILLING

3 ounces (almost ½ brick) full-fat cream cheese

3 heaping tablespoons orange marmalade

TOOLS

Zester or box grater (use the small holes)

Standard 12-cup muffin pan

CONTINUED ON NEXT PAGE

Cupcake liners (optional)

Measuring cups and spoons

Glass measuring cup

Fork or small whisk

2 small bowls

Stand mixer fitted with paddle attachment and whisk attachment or large bowl and electric beaters

Silicone spatula

#20 ice-cream scoop with spring release

Oven mitts

Wire rack

Paring knife

Spoon

Knife or offset spatula

TO MAKE THE CUPCAKES AND FROSTING

1. Preheat the oven. Set the oven to 350°F. Line a muffin pan with paper liners, or grease the inside of each cup with cooking spray or butter (see page 5).

2. Prepare the wet ingredients. In a glass measuring cup with a spout, combine the buttermilk, orange juice, and vanilla. Using a fork or small whisk, stir to combine.

3. Prepare the dry ingredients. In a small bowl, whisk the flour, baking powder, baking soda, and salt to combine fully.

4. Cream the butter. In the bowl of a stand mixer fitted with the paddle attachment, or a large bowl using electric beaters, cream together the butter and sugar on medium-high speed for about 3 minutes until fluffy. Stop the mixer and use a spatula to scrape down the sides of the bowl.

5. Add the orange flavorings. Add the orange zest and orange marmalade to the butter mixture. Mix for 30 seconds. Stop and scrape down the bowl.

6. Add the eggs. Crack 1 egg into a small bowl (if you get any shell in it, see page 5 for tips on easily removing it). Add the egg to the butter mixture. Mix on medium speed for 1 minute. Stop the mixer and use a spatula to scrape down the sides of the bowl. Repeat with the remaining 2 eggs, beating for 1 minute after each addition. Scrape down the bowl.

7. Combine the ingredients. Add half the flour mixture to the bowl and start the mixer on low speed. Add half the buttermilk mixture. Repeat with the flour

CONTINUED ON NEXT PAGE

and buttermilk mixtures until everything is combined. When all the flour mixture is just mixed in, stop the mixer. Use a spatula to scrape down the sides one more time.

8. **Fill the pan.** Using an ice-cream scoop, divide the batter evenly among the prepared cups, filling each about three-quarters full.

9. **Bake.** Carefully place the pan onto the center rack of the preheated oven. Bake for 15 to 18 minutes, rotating the pan halfway through baking (use oven mitts!) so your cupcakes bake evenly. The cupcakes are ready when you can press on the top of them with your finger and the cake springs back (ask an adult to help).

10. **Let cool.** Remove the pan from the oven (use oven mitts!) and place on a wire rack. Let the cupcakes cool in the pan for 10 minutes. Once they're cool enough to touch, remove the cupcakes from the pan and transfer them to the wire rack to cool completely, about 1 hour.

11. **Make the frosting.** While the cupcakes are cooling, make the fruity buttercream following the directions on page 129.

TO MAKE THE FILLING

12. **Prepare the orange filling.** While the cupcakes are cooling, wash the bowl for the stand mixer or beaters and use the whisk attachment, or electric beaters, to whip together the cream cheese and marmalade. Refrigerate your orange filling while the cupcakes cool.

13. **Assemble the cupcakes.** Ask an adult to help you cut a cone shape out of the top of each cupcake. Trim off the bottom (pointy) part of the cones. Use a tiny spoon to place a dollop of the orange filling inside the hole and place the tops back on.

14. **Frost the cupcakes.** Once the cupcakes are filled, use a knife, offset spatula, or a piping bag to spread an even layer of frosting on top of each cupcake.

Decorating Tip: Add an orange slice or the zest of an additional orange to your cupcakes by sprinkling it over the frosting.

Super Baker: This recipe has many steps, but you can do it! Set all your materials and ingredients out ahead of time so you stay organized.

CHOCOLATE CREAM SURPRISE CUPCAKES WITH CHOCOLATE GLAZE

How do you improve on the most famous cupcake in the world, the Hostess Cupcake? Make it fresh at home! To re-create that sweet velvety cupcake, we use two kinds of chocolate and two tricks for adding moisture: yogurt and oil. The result is a cupcake that's rich but firm enough to handle the filling—a simple combination of marshmallow crème, butter, and powdered sugar. Top the whole thing with a thin layer of two-ingredient chocolate glaze. If you *really* want to impress, add a swirl of white curlicues on top.

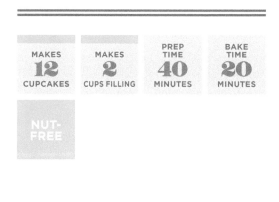

MAKES **12** CUPCAKES

MAKES **2** CUPS FILLING

PREP TIME **40** MINUTES

BAKE TIME **20** MINUTES

NUT-FREE

FOR THE CUPCAKES

Nonstick cooking spray, or unsalted butter for preparing the pan (optional)

⅓ cup semisweet chocolate chips

½ cup unsweetened cocoa powder

½ cup boiling water

1 cup all-purpose flour

½ teaspoon baking soda

¼ teaspoon fine salt

¾ cup sugar

½ cup plain Greek yogurt

½ cup vegetable oil

1 teaspoon pure vanilla extract

2 large eggs

1 batch Chocolate Glaze (page 134)

1 (4.25-ounce) tube white frosting with a pointed tip (optional)

FOR THE FILLING

1½ cups marshmallow crème

8 tablespoons (1 stick) unsalted butter, at room temperature

½ cup powdered sugar

TOOLS

Standard 12-cup muffin pan

Cupcake liners (optional)

Measuring cups and spoons

Mixing bowls

CONTINUED ON NEXT PAGE

Whisk

Stand mixer fitted with paddle attachment or large bowl and electric beaters

Small bowl

Silicone spatula

#20 ice-cream scoop with spring release

Oven mitts

Wire rack

Paring knife

Spoon

Large spoon or offset spatula

TO MAKE THE CUPCAKES AND GLAZE

1. **Preheat the oven.** Set the oven to 325°F. Line a muffin pan with paper liners, or grease the inside of each cup with cooking spray or butter (see page 5).

2. **Melt the chocolate chips.** In a medium bowl, combine the chocolate chips and cocoa powder. Ask an adult to help you pour the hot water over the top. Stir VERY slowly with the whisk to melt the chocolate chips completely. Set aside.

3. **Prepare the dry ingredients.** In a large bowl, whisk the flour, baking soda, and salt to combine well.

4. **Prepare the wet ingredients.** In the bowl of a stand mixer fitted with the paddle attachment, or a large bowl using electric beaters, combine the sugar, Greek yogurt, oil, and vanilla. Beat on medium speed for about 2 minutes until smooth.

5. **Add the eggs.** Crack 1 egg into a small bowl (if you get any shell in it, see page 5 for tips on easily removing it). Add the egg to the butter mixture. Mix on medium speed for 1 minute. Stop the mixer and use a spatula to scrape down the sides of the bowl. Repeat with the remaining egg, mixing for 1 minute more.

6. **Add the flour and chocolate to the wet ingredients.** Carefully pour half the melted chocolate mixture into the bowl and mix on low speed for only 10 seconds. Add half the flour mixture and mix for 10 seconds more. Repeat until all the ingredients are in the bowl and beat until just combined. Do not overmix!

7. **Fill the pan.** Using an ice-cream scoop, divide the batter evenly among the prepared cups, filling each about three-quarters full.

8. **Bake.** Carefully place the pan onto the center rack of the preheated oven. Bake for 18 to 20 minutes, rotating the

pan halfway through baking (use oven mitts!) so your cupcakes bake evenly. The cupcakes are ready when you can press on the top of them with your finger and the cake springs back (ask an adult to help).

9. Let cool. Remove the pan from the oven (use oven mitts!) and place on a wire rack. Let the cupcakes cool in the pan for 10 minutes. Once they're cool enough to touch, remove the cupcakes from the pan and transfer them to the wire rack to cool completely, about 1 hour.

10. Make the glaze. While the cupcakes are cooling, make the chocolate glaze following the directions on page 134.

TO MAKE THE FILLING

11. Make the filling. While the cupcakes are cooling, wash the bowl and paddle attachment or beaters and combine the marshmallow crème and butter in it. Beat on medium speed for about 2 minutes until fluffy. Turn the mixer to low speed and slowly add the powdered sugar. Once all the sugar is in the bowl, increase the speed to medium-high and beat for about 2 minutes until fluffy. Set aside.

12. Assemble the cupcakes. Ask an adult to help cut a cone shape out of each cupcake. Trim off the bottom (pointy) part of the cones. Use a tiny spoon to place a dollop of the crème filling inside the hole and place the tops back on.

13. Glaze the cupcakes. Use a large spoon or offset spatula to spread the chocolate glaze over the top of each cupcake. Let cool for 10 minutes. If using, swirl the white frosting on top in a curlicue shape.

Change It Up: Make the filling a rainbow! Separate the marshmallow mixture into three little bowls. Add a couple drops of food coloring, different colors in each bowl, and stir to blend. Fill each cupcake with one color of filling, or swirl the colors together.

STOLE MY HEART CHOCOLATE CUPCAKES WITH STRAWBERRY PUDDING FILLING

The fun part of these cupcakes is the heart-shaped cutout on top. Get the look like this: Bake the cupcakes, then slice the whole top off each one and use a cookie cutter to punch out a heart. Add a thick layer of filling to the cupcake stump, then replace the top with the heart cutout. Bonus: Use pistachio pudding for a Grinch heart or replace the heart with a star cookie cutter on the Fourth of July. The method works for many occasions—and they're all delicious.

MAKES **12** CUPCAKES

MAKES **2** CUPS FILLING

PREP TIME **40** MINUTES

BAKE TIME **18** MINUTES

NUT-FREE

FOR THE CUPCAKES

Nonstick cooking spray, or unsalted butter for preparing the pan (optional)

1 cup all-purpose flour

½ teaspoon baking soda

½ teaspoon fine salt

¾ cup whole milk

½ cup unsweetened cocoa powder

3 large eggs

1 cup sugar

¾ cup vegetable oil

1 teaspoon pure vanilla extract

Powdered sugar, for dusting

FOR THE FILLING

½ (3.4-ounce package) instant vanilla pudding

1 cup heavy (whipping) cream

2 tablespoons strawberry jam

1 or 2 drops red food coloring

TOOLS

Standard 12-cup muffin pan

Cupcake liners (optional)

Measuring cups and spoons

Large bowl

Whisk

Microwave-safe bowl

Stand mixer fitted with whisk attachment or large bowl and electric beaters

Small bowl

Silicone spatula

#20 ice-cream scoop with spring release

Oven mitts

Wire rack

Paring knife

Small heart-shaped cookie cutter

Sifter or fine-mesh sieve

TO MAKE THE CUPCAKES

1. Preheat the oven. Set the oven to 375°F. Line a muffin pan with paper liners, or grease the inside of each cup with cooking spray or butter (see page 5).

2. Prepare the dry ingredients. In a large bowl, whisk the flour, baking soda, and salt for about 10 seconds to mix well.

3. Prepare the cocoa mixture. Pour the milk into a microwave-safe bowl and heat on Low power for 45 to 60 seconds until warm (like bathwater). Place the cocoa powder in the bowl of a stand mixer fitted with the whisk attachment, or a large bowl using electric beaters, and pour in the warm milk. Whisk until smooth.

4. Add the eggs. Crack 1 egg into a small bowl (if you get any shell in it, see page 5 for tips on easily removing it). Add the egg to the cocoa mixture. Mix on medium speed for 1 minute. Stop and use a spatula to scrape down the sides of the bowl. Repeat with the remaining 2 eggs, beating for 1 minute after each addition.

5. Add the remaining ingredients. Pour the sugar, oil, and vanilla into the bowl with the chocolate. With the mixer on low speed, slowly add the flour mixture. Stop the mixer when just combined.

6. Fill the pan. Using an ice-cream scoop, divide the batter evenly among the prepared cups, filling each about three-quarters full.

7. Bake. Carefully place the pan onto the center rack of the preheated oven. Bake for 16 to 18 minutes, rotating the pan halfway through baking (use oven mitts!) so your cupcakes bake evenly. The cupcakes are ready when you can press on the top of them with your finger and the cake springs back (ask an adult to help).

8. Let cool. Remove the pan from the oven (use oven mitts!) and place on a wire rack. Let the cupcakes cool in the pan for 10 minutes. Once they're cool enough to touch, remove the cupcakes from the pan and transfer them to the wire rack to cool completely, about 1 hour.

CONTINUED ON NEXT PAGE

STOLE MY HEART CHOCOLATE CUPCAKES WITH STRAWBERRY PUDDING FILLING

CONTINUED

TO MAKE THE FILLING

9. Prepare the strawberry filling. While the cupcakes are cooling, wash out the bowl and whisk attachment or beaters. In the bowl, whip the pudding mix, heavy cream, strawberry jam, and food coloring until it's thick and creamy and stiff peaks form (the filling should hold its shape on a spoon). Refrigerate while the cupcakes cool.

10. Assemble the cupcakes. After the cupcakes have cooled completely, ask an adult to help you gently cut the entire top off each cupcake. Use a small heart-shaped cookie cutter to pierce the center of each cupcake's cutoff top. Set the heart cutout aside to enjoy separately. Spread 2 to 3 tablespoons of strawberry filling on the cut cupcakes. Replace the tops of the cupcakes. Just before serving, sprinkle with powdered sugar (use a sifter or small fine-mesh sieve).

Decorating Tip: A light dusting of powdered sugar transforms the look of not just these cupcakes but almost any dessert. Remember, powdered sugar will soak into most cakes over time, so add it at the last minute.

BUTTERBEER CUPCAKES WITH BUTTERSCOTCH FROSTING

Bake-a-ram-us! If you love Harry Potter, these cupcakes are for you. Haven't you always wanted to try butterbeer? This recipe brings that caramel-butterscotch flavor to life! My favorite way to top them is by making golden snitches to perch on top: Use white candy melts in a piping bag to make wing shapes. Let them set up, then place a gold-covered chocolate in the center of your frosted cupcake. Nestle a set of wings on each side . . . and let the games begin!

MAKES	MAKES	PREP TIME	BAKE TIME
12 CUPCAKES	**1½** CUPS FILLING	**40** MINUTES	**22** MINUTES

NUT-FREE

FOR THE CUPCAKES

1½ cups all-purpose flour

¾ cup packed light brown sugar

½ teaspoon baking soda

½ teaspoon baking powder

¼ teaspoon fine salt

⅓ cup vegetable oil

⅓ cup buttermilk

1 teaspoon pure vanilla extract

2 large eggs

⅓ cup cream soda

1 cup toffee bits (without chocolate coating)

¾ cup butterscotch chips

1 batch Whipped Butterbeer Frosting (see Whipped Cream Frosting, Star Baker tip, page 130)

FOR THE FILLING

1 cup butterscotch chips

½ cup heavy (whipping) cream

TOOLS

Standard 12-cup muffin pan

Cupcake liners

Measuring cups and spoons

Mixing bowls

Whisk

Stand mixer fitted with paddle attachment or large bowl and electric beaters

CONTINUED ON NEXT PAGE

Small bowl

Silicone spatula

#20 ice-cream scoop with spring release

Oven mitts

Wire rack

Small microwave-safe bowl

Paring knife

Spoon

Knife or offset spatula

TO MAKE THE CUPCAKES AND FROSTING

1. **Preheat the oven.** Preheat the oven to 350°F. Line a muffin pan with paper liners, or grease the inside of each cup with cooking spray or butter (see page 5).

2. **Prepare the dry ingredients.** In a large bowl, whisk the flour, brown sugar, baking soda, baking powder, and salt for about 10 seconds until well mixed. Set aside.

3. **Prepare the wet ingredients.** In the bowl of a stand mixer fitted with the paddle attachment, or a large bowl using electric beaters, combine the oil, buttermilk, and vanilla. Crack 1 egg into a small bowl (if you get any shell in it, see page 5 for tips on easily removing it). Add the egg to the buttermilk mixture. Repeat with the remaining egg.

Mix on medium speed for about 20 seconds until smooth. Stop the mixer and use a silicone spatula to scrape down the sides of the bowl.

4. **Combine the ingredients.** With the mixer on low speed, slowly add half the buttermilk mixture and beat for 10 seconds. Add half the flour mixture and beat for 10 seconds more. Add half the cream soda and beat for 10 seconds. Repeat until all the ingredients are in the bowl, beating for 10 seconds after each addition. Stop the mixer and use a silicone spatula to scrape down the sides of the bowl.

5. **Add the buttery flavors.** Pour the toffee bits and butterscotch chips into the batter. Using a silicone spatula, gently stir to mix in.

6. **Fill the pan.** Using an ice-cream scoop, divide the batter evenly among the prepared cups, filling each about three-quarters full.

7. **Bake.** Carefully place the pan onto the center rack of the preheated oven. Bake for 18 to 22 minutes, rotating the pan halfway through baking (use oven mitts!) so your cupcakes bake evenly. The cupcakes are ready when you can press on the top of them with your finger and the cake springs back (ask an adult to help).

8. Let cool. Remove the pan from the oven (use oven mitts!) and place on a wire rack. Let the cupcakes cool in the pan for 10 minutes. Once they're cool enough to touch, remove the cupcakes from the pan and transfer them to the wire rack to cool completely, about 1 hour.

9. Make the frosting. While the cupcakes are cooling, make the whipped butterbeer frosting following the directions on page 130.

TO MAKE THE FILLING

10. Make the caramel filling. While the cupcakes are cooling, place the butterscotch chips and heavy cream in a microwave-safe bowl and heat on High power for 10 seconds at a time until the chips are soft enough to stir (ask an adult to help, if needed). Using a silicone spatula, mix thoroughly until smooth. Set aside.

11. Assemble the cupcakes. After the cupcakes have cooled completely, ask an adult to help you cut a cone shape out of the top of each cupcake. Trim off the bottom (pointy) part of the cones. Use a tiny spoon to place a dollop of the caramel filling inside the hole and place the tops back on.

12. Frost the cupcakes. Once the cupcakes are filled, use a knife or offset spatula to spread an even layer of frosting on top of each cupcake. Because the liners won't show up very well after baking, consider adding a second liner for better presentation.

Change It Up: Love caramel sauce? Ask an adult to help you: Place 1 (14-ounce) unopened can of sweetened condensed milk in a large saucepan or slow cooker with enough water to cover it completely. Gently boil over low heat for 3 hours. (Check every hour to make sure water still covers the can. If not, add more water.) Let cool. When you open the can, it'll be rich and velvety. Drizzle the caramel over the cupcakes. Transfer leftovers to a small container with a lid and refrigerate for up to 3 weeks. Bonus: This caramel makes an amazing dip for fresh apple slices!

chapter 4

BIRTHDAY PARTY IDEAS

Time to celebrate! From adorable bears bobbing on ocean waves to rainbows and campfires, these 10 decorating tips will make your party even sweeter.

Need more photos? Visit my website at Foodlets.com/cupcakes for pictures of each recipe.

OREO DIRT CUPS (WITH COOKIES & CREAM CUPCAKES)

Crushed Oreos make the most delicious dirt for bulldozers, dinosaurs, gummy worms, or anything else you can dream up! Want cookies inside and out? We're adding crushed Oreos to the prepared batter to make Cookies & Cream Cupcakes.

MAKES **12** CUPCAKES	PREP TIME **30** MINUTES	BAKE TIME **20** MINUTES	DECORATING TIME **30** MINUTES

NUT-FREE

FOR THE CUPCAKES

Nonstick cooking spray (optional)

8 tablespoons (1 stick) unsalted butter, at room temperature, plus more for preparing the pan (optional)

1 cup sugar

1½ cups all-purpose flour

1½ teaspoons baking powder

½ teaspoon fine salt

½ cup whole milk

1 teaspoon pure vanilla extract

2 large eggs

1 cup crushed Oreos (about 12 cookies)

1 batch Chocolate Buttercream (page 135)

FOR THE DECORATION

Oreo cookies

Gummy worms, halved; small dinosaurs; or small bulldozers

TOOLS

Standard 12-cup muffin pan

Cupcake liners (optional)

Measuring cups and spoons

Stand mixer fitted with paddle attachment or large bowl and electric beaters

Silicone spatula

Mixing bowls

Whisk or fork

Glass measuring cup

Small bowl

#20 ice-cream scoop with spring release

Oven mitts

Wire rack

Food processor or resealable bag and rolling pin

Plate

Knife or offset spatula

TO MAKE THE CUPCAKES AND FROSTING

1. Preheat the oven. Set the oven to 350°F. Line a muffin pan with paper liners, or grease the inside of each cup with cooking spray or butter (see page 5).

2. Cream the butter. In the bowl of a stand mixer fitted with the paddle attachment, or a large bowl using electric beaters, cream together the butter and sugar on medium speed for about 3 minutes until fluffy, stopping partway through to scrape down the sides of the bowl with a spatula. Once the butter is fluffy, stop the mixer.

3. Mix the dry ingredients. In a medium bowl, combine the flour, baking powder, and salt. Using a whisk or a fork, stir about 20 times to combine well.

4. Mix the wet ingredients. In a glass measuring cup with a spout, combine the milk and vanilla.

5. Add the eggs. Crack 1 egg into a small bowl (if you get any shell in it, see page 5 for tips on easily removing it). Add the egg to the butter mixture. Mix on medium speed for 1 minute. Stop the mixer and use the spatula to scrape down the sides of the bowl. Repeat with the remaining egg. Mix for 1 minute. Stop and scrape again.

6. Add the dry ingredients to the wet ingredients. Pour half the flour mixture into the egg mixture. Mix on low speed for 10 seconds. Add half the milk mixture. Mix for 10 seconds more. Add the remaining flour and milk mixtures, mixing for 10 seconds between each addition. Using the spatula, scrape down the sides of the bowl. Fold (stir down, over, and up again, repeating in a circle) in the crushed Oreos.

7. Fill the pan. Using an ice-cream scoop, divide the batter evenly among the prepared cups, filling each about three-quarters full.

8. Bake. Carefully place the pan onto the center rack of the preheated oven. Bake for 18 to 20 minutes, rotating the pan halfway through baking (use oven mitts!) so your cupcakes bake evenly. The cupcakes are ready when you can press on the top of them with your finger and the cake springs back (ask an adult to help).

CONTINUED ON NEXT PAGE

9. Let cool. Remove the pan from the oven (use oven mitts!) and place on a wire rack. Let the cupcakes cool in the pan for 10 minutes. Once they're cool enough to touch, remove the cupcakes from the pan and transfer them to the wire rack to cool completely, about 1 hour.

10. Make the frosting. While the cupcakes are cooling, make the chocolate buttercream following the directions on page 135.

TO DECORATE

11. Make the dirt. Place the Oreos in the food processor and pulse until broken into small pieces (alternatively, place them in a resealable bag and crush with a rolling pin). Pour the "dirt" onto a plate. Set aside.

12. Frost the cupcakes. Once the cupcakes are completely cooled, using a knife or small offset spatula, frost each cupcake right to the edges.

13. Roll in the dirt and add decorations. Gently roll the frosted tops of the cupcakes in the "dirt" until completely covered. Top with two halves of gummy worms, a dinosaur, or a bulldozer.

★ **Star Baker:** Oreo cookies have been on the market since 1912, when their fiercest competition was animal crackers! Today's cookies, made with a special ratio of 79 percent cookie to 21 percent cream filling, are the most popular in the world.

CONFETTI CUPCAKES
FOUR FUN WAYS TO USE SPRINKLES

What do you call sprinkles when they're baked inside a cupcake? Confetti! Make your own confetti cupcakes using vanilla cupcakes and a ton of sprinkles, inside and out. Top with Vanilla Buttercream (page 128) and choose one—or all!—of the following decorating ideas.

MAKES	PREP TIME	BAKE TIME	DECORATING TIME
12 CUPCAKES	**30** MINUTES	**20** MINUTES	**20** MINUTES

NUT-FREE

FOR THE CUPCAKES

Nonstick cooking spray (optional)

8 tablespoons (1 stick) unsalted butter, at room temperature, plus more for preparing the pan (optional)

1 cup sugar

1½ cups all-purpose flour

1½ teaspoons baking powder

½ teaspoon fine salt

½ cup whole milk

1 teaspoon pure vanilla extract

2 large eggs

1 cup multicolored sprinkles

1 batch Vanilla Buttercream (page 128)

FOR THE DECORATION

Multicolored sprinkles

TOOLS

Standard 12-cup muffin pan

Cupcake liners (optional)

Measuring bowls and spoons

Stand mixer fitted with paddle attachment or large bowl and electric beaters

Silicone spatula

2 small bowls

Glass measuring cup

Whisk or fork

CONTINUED ON NEXT PAGE

#20 ice-cream scoop with spring release

Oven mitts

Wire rack

Pastry bag or resealable bag (optional)

Knife or offset spatula (optional)

Small plate (optional)

Small cookie cutter (optional)

TO MAKE THE CUPCAKES AND FROSTING

1. Preheat the oven. Set the oven to 350°F. Line a muffin pan with paper liners, or grease the inside of each cup with cooking spray or butter (see page 5).

2. Cream the butter. In the bowl of a stand mixer fitted with the paddle attachment, or a large bowl using electric beaters, cream together the butter and sugar on medium speed for about 3 minutes until fluffy, stopping partway through to scrape down the sides of the bowl with a spatula. Once the butter is fluffy, stop the mixer.

3. Mix the dry ingredients. In a small bowl, combine the flour, baking powder, and salt. Using a whisk or a fork, stir about 20 times to combine well.

4. Mix the wet ingredients. In a glass measuring cup with a spout, combine the milk and vanilla. Stir well and set aside.

5. Add the eggs. Crack 1 egg into a small bowl (if you get any shell in it, see page 5 for tips on easily removing it). Add the egg to the butter mixture. Mix on medium speed for 1 minute. Using a spatula, scrape down the sides of the bowl. Repeat with the remaining egg. Mix for 1 minute. Stop and scrape down the bowl again.

6. Add the dry ingredients to the wet ingredients. Pour half the flour mixture into the butter mixture. Mix on low speed for 10 seconds. Add half the milk mixture. Mix on low speed for 10 seconds more. Add the remaining flour and milk mixtures, mixing for 10 seconds between each addition. Stop the mixer and using the spatula, scrape down the sides of the bowl. Stir the batter a few more times just until you can't see any flour.

7. Add the red sprinkles. Using the silicone spatula, fold (stir down, over, and up again, repeating in a circle) the sprinkles into the batter.

8. Fill the pan. Using an ice-cream scoop, divide the batter evenly among the prepared cups, filling each about three-quarters full.

9. Bake. Carefully place the pan onto the center rack of the preheated oven. Bake for 18 to 20 minutes, rotating the pan halfway through baking (use oven mitts!) so your cupcakes bake evenly. The cupcakes are ready when you can press on the top of them with your finger and the cake springs back (ask an adult to help).

10. **Let cool.** Remove the pan from the oven (use oven mitts!) and place on a wire rack. Let the cupcakes cool in the pan for 10 minutes. Once they're cool enough to touch, remove the cupcakes from the pan and transfer them to the wire rack to cool completely, about 1 hour.

11. **Make the frosting.** While the cupcakes are cooling, make the vanilla buttercream following the directions on page 128.

4 WAYS TO DECORATE

1. **Sprinkles on top:** Fill a pastry bag (or resealable bag with a corner tip snipped off) with frosting. Add a big swirl of frosting to the top of each cupcake. Sprinkle with any colorful combination of candy confetti you like. Pro tip: You'll have better control if you pour the sprinkles into your hand and use your fingers to let them fall onto the cupcakes, rather than shaking them straight from the container.

2. **Rim of sprinkles:** Using a knife or offset spatula, spread a big mound of frosting on top of each cupcake. Flatten the top to create a thick edge of frosting. Pour sprinkles onto a small plate, then roll just the frosted edges of each cupcake in the sprinkles. The tops should remain plain with the edges covered in sprinkles.

3. **Dip o' sprinkles:** Using a knife or offset spatula, spread a big mound of frosting on top of each cupcake. Flatten the tops to create a thick edge of frosting. Pour sprinkles onto a small plate, and then gently dip the very tops of the frosted cupcakes into the sprinkles. The tops should be covered in sprinkles, and the edges will be plain.

4. **Cookie cutter sprinkles:** Using a knife or offset spatula, spread a big mound of frosting on top of each cupcake. Flatten the tops to create a thick edge of frosting. Place your favorite small cookie cutter—such as a heart, flower, or star—in the center. Pour the sprinkles inside the cookie cutter, and then gently pull the cookie cutter up to reveal your design.

Ask an Adult: Always get help using the oven. You may also want advice on how to organize your frosting and sprinkles.

MARSHMALLOW FLOWERS

You'll never believe how such an easy technique can have such beautiful results! My four-year-old made these for her own birthday party, and they were perfect. Use any color of sparkles or a combination of colors, and in the center of your cupcakes, add a pudding cream filling with a drop of food coloring to match the sparkles on the outside. I like lemon cupcakes because the fresh flavor matches well with the flowers, but feel free to use any cupcake you like from chapters 2 and 3!

FOR THE CUPCAKES

1 batch Lemon Cupcakes (page 35)
1 batch Vanilla Buttercream (page 128)
or Cream Cheese Frosting (page 131)
1 batch Boston Cream Filling (optional; see page 49)

FOR THE DECORATION

Cake sparkles
Mini marshmallows

TOOLS

Paring knife (optional)
Small spoon (optional)
Knife or offset spatula
Small plate
Kitchen shears

MAKES **12** CUPCAKES

PREP TIME **30** MINUTES

BAKE TIME **20** MINUTES

DECORATING TIME **40** MINUTES

NUT-FREE

TO MAKE THE CUPCAKES, FILLING, AND FROSTING

1. Make the cupcakes. Make the lemon cupcakes following the directions on page 35. Let cool completely, about 1 hour.

2. Make the filling (if using). While the cupcakes are cooling, make the Boston cream filling following the directions on page 49.

3. Make the frosting. While the cupcakes are cooling, make the vanilla buttercream following the directions on page 128.

4. Add the filling (if using). Ask an adult to help you cut a cone shape out of the top of each cupcake. Cut off the bottom (pointy) part of the cones. Use a tiny spoon to place a dollop of the cream filling inside each hole and place the tops back on.

5. Frost the cupcakes. Once the cupcakes are completely cooled, using a knife or offset spatula, spread a thick layer of frosting on top of each cupcake.

TO DECORATE

6. Prepare the decorations. Pour the sparkles onto a small plate or into a bowl. Use kitchen shears to cut the mini marshmallows in half diagonally. Press the cut side of each marshmallow into the sparkles.

7. Assemble the flowers. Gently press the rounded side of a marshmallow in the center of a cupcake with the sparkle-side up. Repeat in a round pattern to form flowers.

⭐ **Star Baker:** Marshmallows are made out of four ingredients: sugar, gelatin, water, and . . . air!

FRESH FISH WITH COLORFUL CANDY SCALES

Got a summer party coming up? These are for you! All you need are M&Ms (or any colored candies) to make the cutest fish in—or out—of the sea. Use all one color for your "fins," or alternate rows. It's all up to you. Chocolate cupcakes are wonderful because they add a flavor bomb when you bite into an M&M on top, but the choice of cupcakes is all yours.

MAKES	PREP TIME	BAKE TIME	DECORATING TIME
12 CUPCAKES	**10** MINUTES	**20** MINUTES	**30** MINUTES

NUT-FREE

FOR THE CUPCAKES

1 batch Chocolate Cupcakes (page 31)

1 batch Vanilla Buttercream (page 128) or Cream Cheese Frosting (page 131)

FOR THE DECORATION

Yellow, blue, and green food coloring, or colors of choice
1 (1-pound) bag M&Ms
Candy eyeballs

TOOLS

7 small bowls
Spoons
Knife or offset spatula

TO MAKE THE CUPCAKES AND FROSTING

1. Make the cupcakes. Make the chocolate cupcakes following the instructions on page 31. Let cool completely, about 1 hour.

2. Prepare the frosting. While the cupcakes are cooling, make the vanilla buttercream or cream cheese frosting following the directions on page 128 or page 131.

TO DECORATE

3. Color the frosting. If you want 3 different colors of cupcakes, evenly divide the frosting among 3 small bowls. To each bowl, add 2 or 3 drops of your choice of food coloring. Stir well.

4. Frost the cupcakes. Once the cupcakes are completely cooled, use a knife or offset spatula to spread an even layer of frosting on top of each cupcake

5. Sort the M&Ms. Sort the candies by color and decide which color, or color combinations, you'll use (*psst* . . . blue, yellow, and green work best if those are the frosting colors you chose). Sort the red M&Ms into a separate pile to use for lips.

6. Assemble the fish. On top of each cupcake, place a candy eyeball just to the left of the center. To form the lips, add 2 red M&Ms on their sides, just to the left and slightly underneath the eye (so it completes the side of the fish's face). Add the "scales" by arranging M&Ms on their sides, in slightly curved vertical rows to the right of the lips. Repeat the M&M rows, using fewer and fewer M&Ms for each row, until the "fish" is half-covered.

Ask an Adult: Get help with the food coloring. Always start with only a drop or two. You can add more coloring but you can never take it out if you put in too much.

MELTING ICE-CREAM CONES

The best thing about these cupcake ice-cream cones is that they don't really melt! Use a scoop of frosting for the "ice cream" and your cones will stay put. Strawberry is a delicious flavor with the chocolate and vanilla toppings but you can use any cupcake recipe you like.

MAKES	PREP TIME	BAKE TIME	DECORATING TIME
12 CUPCAKES	**30** MINUTES	**20** MINUTES	**30** MINUTES

NUT-FREE

FOR THE CUPCAKES

1 batch Strawberry Cupcakes (page 23)

1 batch Vanilla Buttercream (page 128)

FOR THE DECORATION

1 (7-ounce) container dipping chocolate
12 old-fashioned ice-cream cones
Sprinkles

TOOLS

Spoon
#20 ice-cream scoop with spring release
Kitchen shears

TO MAKE THE CUPCAKES AND FROSTING

1. Make the cupcakes. Make the strawberry cupcakes following the instructions on page 23. Let cool completely, about 1 hour.

2. Make the frosting. While the cupcakes are cooling, make the vanilla buttercream following the directions on page 128. Set aside.

TO DECORATE

3. Melt the chocolate and start decorating. Remove the lid and foil from the dipping chocolate container. Place the container in the microwave and heat on High power for 30 seconds. Stir well and repeat heating in 30-second increments until the chocolate is smooth. Using a spoon, drizzle a thick layer of melted chocolate on top of each cooled cupcake (it should look uneven and drippy).

4. Add the "ice cream." Using an ice-cream scoop, carefully place a scoopful of Vanilla Buttercream on top of the chocolate glaze on each cupcake.

5. Add the ice-cream cone. Using clean kitchen shears, cut the top rims off the ice-cream cones to make them smaller (see Star Baker tip). Perch the miniature ice-cream cone on top of the buttercream "ice cream."

6. Finish decorating. Add sprinkles and more chocolate sauce to the "ice cream."

★ Star Baker: Ask an adult to help trim the ice-cream cones, if needed. It's tricky, so if it doesn't work, don't worry—just use the whole cone!

GATHER 'ROUND THE CAMPFIRE CUPCAKES

Perfect for a sleepover or camping trip, these campfire cupcakes are all fun and no burns. See page viii for photos!

MAKES 12 CUPCAKES

PREP TIME 30 MINUTES

BAKE TIME 20 MINUTES

DECORATING TIME 30 MINUTES

NUT-FREE

FOR THE FLAMING CUPCAKES

Nonstick cooking spray (optional)

8 tablespoons (1 stick) unsalted butter, melted, plus more for preparing the pan (optional)

1¼ cups all-purpose flour

½ teaspoon baking powder

½ teaspoon baking soda

½ teaspoon fine salt

½ teaspoon ground cinnamon

¼ teaspoon ground nutmeg

¼ teaspoon ground ginger

1 cup packed light brown sugar

½ cup full-fat sour cream

1 teaspoon pure vanilla extract

2 large eggs

1 (about 3-ounce) jar red sprinkles

1 batch Vanilla Buttercream (page 128)

FOR THE DECORATION

Yellow food coloring
Red Hots cinnamon candies
Pretzel sticks
Mini marshmallows
Toothpicks

TOOLS

Standard 12-cup muffin pan
Cupcake liners (optional)
Measuring cups and spoons

Mixing bowls

Whisk or fork

Stand mixer fitted with paddle attachment or large bowl and electric beaters

Small bowl

Silicone spatula

#20 ice-cream scoop with spring release

Oven mitts

Wire rack

Knife or offset spatula

TO MAKE THE CUPCAKES AND FROSTING

1. Preheat the oven. Set the oven to 350°F. Line a muffin pan with paper liners, or grease the inside of each cup with cooking spray or butter (see page 5).

2. Mix the dry ingredients. In a medium bowl, combine the flour, baking powder, baking soda, salt, cinnamon, nutmeg, and ginger. Using a whisk or a fork, stir about 20 times to combine well.

3. Cream the butter. In the bowl of a stand mixer fitted with the paddle attachment, or a large bowl using electric beaters, cream together the melted butter, brown sugar, sour cream, and vanilla on medium speed until smooth.

4. Add the eggs. Crack 1 egg into a small bowl (if you get any shell in it, see page 5 for tips on easily removing it). Add the egg to the butter mixture. Mix on medium speed for 30 seconds. Stop the mixer and use the spatula to scrape down the sides of the bowl. Repeat with the remaining egg and mix for 30 seconds more.

5. Add the dry ingredients to the wet ingredients. Pour half the flour mixture into the butter mixture. Mix on low speed for 10 seconds. Stop the mixer and use the spatula to scrape down the sides of the bowl. Add the remaining flour. Mix for 10 seconds more. Using the spatula, scrape down the sides of the bowl. Stir the batter a few more times just until you can't see any flour.

6. Add the red sprinkles. Using the silicone spatula, fold (stir down, over, and up again, repeating in a circle) the sprinkles into the batter.

7. Fill the pan. Using an ice-cream scoop, divide the batter evenly among the prepared cups, filling each about three-quarters full.

8. Bake. Carefully place the pan onto the center rack of the preheated oven. Bake for 18 to 20 minutes, rotating the pan halfway through baking (use oven mitts!) so your cupcakes bake evenly. The cupcakes are ready when you can press on the top of them with your finger and the cake springs back (ask an adult to help).

CONTINUED ON NEXT PAGE

9. Let cool. Remove the pan from the oven (use oven mitts!) and place on a wire rack. Let the cupcakes cool in the pan for 10 minutes. Once they're cool enough to touch, remove the cupcakes from the pan and transfer them to the wire rack to cool completely, about 1 hour.

10. Make the frosting. While the cupcakes are cooling, make the vanilla buttercream following the directions on page 128.

TO DECORATE

11. Color the frosting. Add 2 or 3 drops of yellow food coloring to the vanilla buttercream and mix until the color is uniform.

12. Frost the cupcakes. Once the cupcakes are completely cooled, use a knife or offset spatula to spread an even layer of frosting on top of each cupcake.

13. Make the "fire." Arrange 3 to 5 Red Hots candies in the center of each cupcake. In a circle around the candies, place 5 or 6 pretzel sticks against one another to resemble a tepee.

14. Add the "roasting sticks." Thread 1 or 2 mini marshmallows onto each of 12 toothpicks (like you do when you are going to roast marshmallows over the fire). Insert one "roasting stick" per cupcake, just to one side of each "fire."

SPORTY CUPCAKES THREE WAYS
FOOTBALLS, BASKETBALLS, AND BASEBALLS

If you're into sports, you'll love these sports-themed cupcakes. The decorations are similar for each ball, with key changes. I use chocolate cupcakes with this recipe, but you can bake any flavor you like. You'll decorate each ball with white, black, or red frosting; you can find small tubes in the colors you need at most grocery stores.

MAKES	PREP TIME	BAKE TIME	DECORATING TIME
12 CUPCAKES	**30** MINUTES	**20** MINUTES	**30** MINUTES

NUT-FREE

FOR THE CUPCAKES

1 batch Chocolate Cupcakes (page 31)

FOR THE FOOTBALLS

1 batch Chocolate Buttercream (page 135)
1 (4.25-ounce) tube white frosting

FOR THE BASKETBALLS

1 batch Cream Cheese Frosting (page 131) or Vanilla Buttercream (page 128)
Orange food coloring
1 (4.25-ounce) tube black frosting

FOR THE BASEBALLS

1 batch Cream Cheese Frosting (page 131) or Vanilla Buttercream (page 128)
1 (4.25-ounce) tube red frosting

TOOLS

Pastry bag fitted with star tip
Knife or offset spatula

TO MAKE THE CUPCAKES

1. **Make the cupcakes.** Make the chocolate cupcakes following the

CONTINUED ON NEXT PAGE

instructions on page 31. Let cool completely, about 1 hour.

TO MAKE THE FOOTBALLS

2. Make the frosting. While the cupcakes are cooling, make the chocolate buttercream following the directions on page 135.

3. Create the football shapes. Fill a pastry bag fitted with the star tip with chocolate buttercream. On top of each cupcake, pipe frosting in a zigzag pattern so the center is wider than the ends (to make a football).

4. Add the laces. Use the white frosting to draw a straight line down the center of each cupcake. Finish with 4 short horizontal lines across the straight line to make the football's laces.

TO MAKE THE BASKETBALLS

5. Make the orange frosting. While the cupcakes are cooling, make the cream cheese frosting or vanilla buttercream following the directions on page 131 or page 128. Add orange food coloring (or a combination of yellow and red) to the frosting in small increments, stirring well after each addition, until your reach your desired color.

6. Create the basketball shapes. Using a knife or small offset spatula, spread orange frosting on top of each cupcake.

7. Add the seams. Using the black frosting, squeeze a line down the center of each cupcake, then add 2 curved lines on each side (so it resembles the lines on a basketball).

TO MAKE THE BASEBALLS

8. Make the frosting. While the cupcakes are cooling, make the cream cheese frosting or vanilla buttercream following the directions on page 131 or page 128.

9. Create the baseball shapes. Using a knife or small offset spatula, spread the frosting on top of each cupcake.

10. Add the seams. Using the red frosting, squeeze 2 curved lines on each side of each cupcake. Add short perpendicular lines across each curved line (so it resembles the seams on a baseball).

Ask an Adult: When ready to decorate your cupcakes, ask an adult to show you how to make one, then use it as a guide to decorate the other cupcakes.

COLORFUL COOKIE MONSTERS

These fuzzy monsters are so cute. Use candy eyeballs and a piping bag, both found in the cake decorating section of most large grocery stores. Or add a tiny chocolate chip cookie to create *THE* Cookie Monster. The secret is deeply colored frosting. Want a shortcut? Buy premade frosting already colored in a tube ready to pipe.

MAKES	PREP TIME	BAKE TIME	DECORATING TIME
12 CUPCAKES	**30** MINUTES	**20** MINUTES	**30** MINUTES

NUT-FREE

FOR THE CUPCAKES

Nonstick cooking spray (optional)

8 tablespoons (1 stick) unsalted butter, at room temperature, plus more for preparing the pan (optional)

1½ cups all-purpose flour

2 teaspoons baking powder

½ teaspoon fine salt

1 cup sugar

2 large eggs

½ cup buttermilk

2 teaspoons pure vanilla extract

½ cup mini chocolate chips

1 batch Vanilla Buttercream (page 128)

FOR THE DECORATION

Red, blue, and green food coloring paste

Assorted candy eyeballs

Small chocolate chip cookies (for the Cookie Monster)

TOOLS

Standard 12-cup muffin pan

Cupcake liners (optional)

Measuring cups and spoons

Mixing bowls

Whisk or fork

Stand mixer fitted with paddle attachment or large bowl and electric beaters

CONTINUED ON NEXT PAGE

Silicone spatula

4 small bowls

Glass measuring cup

#20 ice-cream scoop with spring release

Oven mitts

Wire rack

Piping bag fitted with star tip

TO MAKE THE CUPCAKES AND FROSTING

1. Preheat the oven. Set the oven to 350°F. Line a muffin pan with paper liners, or grease the inside of each cup with cooking spray or butter (see page 5).

2. Mix the dry ingredients. In a medium bowl, combine the flour, baking powder, and salt. Using a whisk or a fork, stir about 20 times to combine well. Set aside.

3. Cream the butter. In the bowl of a stand mixer fitted with the paddle attachment, or a large bowl using electric beaters, cream together the butter and sugar on medium speed for about 3 minutes until fluffy, stopping partway through to scrape down the sides of the bowl with a spatula. Once the butter is fluffy, stop the mixer.

4. Add the eggs. Crack 1 egg into a small bowl (if you get any shell in it, see page 5 for tips on easily removing it). Add the egg to the butter mixture. Mix on medium speed for 1 minute. Stop the mixer and use a spatula to scrape down the sides of the bowl. Repeat with the remaining egg, mixing for 1 minute more. Stop the mixer and use the spatula to scrape down the sides of the bowl.

5. Mix the wet ingredients. Pour the buttermilk into a glass measuring cup with a spout. Add the vanilla and stir well.

6. Combine the wet ingredients and the dry ingredients. Pour half the flour mixture into the butter mixture. Beat on low speed for 10 seconds. Add half the buttermilk mixture. Beat on low speed for 10 seconds more. Stop the mixer and use the spatula to scrape down the sides of the bowl. Add the remaining flour and buttermilk mixtures. Beat for 10 seconds more. Using the spatula, scrape down the sides of the bowl. Stir the batter a few more times just until you can't see any flour.

7. Add the chocolate chips. Using the spatula, gently fold (stir down, over, and up again, repeating in a circle) in the chocolate chips.

8. Fill the pan. Using an ice-cream scoop, divide the batter evenly among the prepared cups, filling each about three-quarters full.

9. Bake. Carefully place the pan onto the center rack of the preheated oven. Bake for 18 to 20 minutes, rotating the pan halfway through baking (use oven mitts!) so your cupcakes bake evenly. The cupcakes are ready when you can press on the top of them with your finger and the cake springs back (ask an adult to help).

10. Let cool. Remove the pan from the oven (use oven mitts!) and place on a wire rack. Let the cupcakes cool in the pan for 10 minutes. Once they're cool enough to touch, remove the cupcakes from the pan and transfer them to the wire rack to cool completely, about 1 hour.

11. Make the frosting. While the cupcakes are cooling, make the vanilla buttercream following the directions on page 128.

TO DECORATE

12. Color the frosting. Divide the frosting evenly among 3 small bowls. To one bowl, add the red paste in small increments, stirring well after each addition until you reach your desired color. Repeat with blue and green in the remaining bowls.

13. Create the monster hair. Fill the piping bag with your choice of color. Press the top of the bag to the top of your cupcake, squeeze, and pull up until you have a "strand of hair." Repeat until the cupcake is covered. (Need to make it easier? Frost your cupcakes in a thick, even layer, then use a fork to comb the frosting in all directions, making it look like hair.) Do the same with your blue and green frosting, making as many red, green, or blue hairy monsters as you like.

14. Add the eyeballs. Arrange 1 big eyeball, 3 regular-size eyes, or any combination you like on top of the frosting, where you think the eye(s) look best. To make a Cookie Monster, arrange 2 eyeballs and 1 small chocolate chip cookie where the mouth would be.

♥ **Ask an Adult:** If needed, ask an adult to help you put the frosting in your piping bags. It can sometimes be tricky. Pro tip: Fold the piping bag outward a little to create a cup and keep the outer edges of the bag clean. Even if you start with a tube of store-bought frosting, practice squeezing it out on a piece of parchment paper or aluminum foil.

BEARS ON THE BEACH

Coconut cupcakes give these beachy-keen cupcakes their tropical flavor. The addition of a sweet pineapple filling will make you feel like you've just hit the beach yourself. See page 74 for a photo!

MAKES	PREP TIME	BAKE TIME	DECORATING TIME
12 CUPCAKES	**30** MINUTES	**25** MINUTES	**30** MINUTES

★ **Star Baker:** Use sweetened coconut. The unsweetened kind won't add the flavor you need.

↻ **Change It Up:** Make the whole cupcake a beach! Dip the entire top of the cupcake in the ground graham crackers. Put the umbrella in the "sand," set the ring to the side, and use kitchen shears to make "beach towels" out of fruit leather for the bears to lay on.

FOR THE CUPCAKES

1 batch Coconut Cupcakes (page 18)

1 batch Cream Cheese–Coconut Frosting (page 131)

FOR THE FILLING

1 cup pineapple topping (such as Smucker's)

FOR THE DECORATION

Green and blue food coloring
4 whole graham crackers
Bear-shaped graham crackers
Large ring-shaped gummy candies
Paper cocktail umbrellas

TOOLS

Standard 12-cup muffin pan
Cupcake liners (optional)
Measuring cups and spoons
Stand mixer fitted with paddle attachment or large bowl and electric beaters
Silicone spatula
Mixing bowls
Whisk or fork
Small bowl
#20 ice-cream scoop with spring release
Oven mitts
Wire rack
Paring knife
Spoons

Food processor or resealable bag with rolling pin

Small plate

Knife or offset spatula

TO MAKE THE CUPCAKES AND FROSTING

1. Make the cupcakes. Make the coconut cupcakes following the directions on page 18. Let cool completely, about 1 hour.

2. Make the frosting. While the cupcakes are cooling, make the cream cheese–coconut frosting following the directions on page 131.

TO MAKE THE FILLING

3. Add the filling. Ask an adult to help you cut a cone shape out of the top of each cupcake. Cut off the bottom (pointy) part of the cones. Using a tiny spoon, place a dollop of the pineapple filling inside each hole and place the tops back on.

TO DECORATE

4. Color the frosting. Add 1 drop of green food coloring and 1 drop of blue to the frosting, then mix well to create an ocean blue color. Set aside.

5. Create the sand. In a food processor, pulse the graham crackers (you can also place them in a resealable bag and crush them with a rolling pin) until crushed. Pour the crushed crackers onto a small plate. Set aside.

6. Assemble the beach. Using a knife or offset spatula, frost each cupcake. Carefully dip just half of the frosted top into the crushed graham crackers to form the beach.

7. Finish with a bear. Put each bear-shaped graham inside a gummy ring (it should look like the bears are wearing a floatie). Arrange one bear with a floatie in the "water" on each cupcake. Finish by placing an umbrella on each beach.

A RAINBOW IN THE CLOUDS

If you love rainbows, you'll love these cupcakes with rainbows inside and out! Start with vanilla cupcake batter and just add color. Then top each one with a candy rainbow in the clouds. See page 98 for a photo!

MAKES	PREP TIME	BAKE TIME	DECORATING TIME
12 CUPCAKES	**30** MINUTES	**20** MINUTES	**30** MINUTES

NUT-FREE

FOR THE CUPCAKES

Nonstick cooking spray (optional)

8 tablespoons (1 stick) unsalted butter, at room temperature, plus more for preparing the pan (optional)

1 cup sugar

1½ cups all-purpose flour

1½ teaspoons baking powder

½ teaspoon fine salt

½ cup whole milk

1 teaspoon pure vanilla extract

2 large eggs

Blue, red, and green food coloring

1 batch Vanilla Buttercream (page 128)

FOR THE DECORATION

Blue food coloring

Rainbow candy strips (like Airheads)

Mini marshmallows

TOOLS

Standard 12-cup muffin pan

Cupcake liners (optional)

Measuring cups and spoons

Stand mixer fitted with paddle attachment or large bowl and electric beaters

Silicone spatula

Mixing bowls

Whisk or fork

Glass measuring cup

CONTINUED ON NEXT PAGE

4 small bowls

3 spoons

Toothpicks

Oven mitts

Wire rack

Knife or offset spatula

Kitchen shears

TO MAKE THE CUPCAKES AND FROSTING

1. **Preheat the oven.** Set the oven to 350°F. Line a muffin pan with paper liners, or grease the inside of each cup with cooking spray or butter (see page 5).

2. **Cream the butter.** In the bowl of a stand mixer fitted with the paddle attachment, or a large bowl using electric beaters, cream together the butter and sugar on medium speed for about 3 minutes until fluffy, stopping partway through to scrape down the sides of the bowl with a spatula. Once the butter is fluffy, stop the mixer.

3. **Mix the dry ingredients.** In another large bowl, combine the flour, baking powder, and salt. Using a whisk or a fork, stir about 20 times to combine well.

4. **Mix the wet ingredients.** Pour the milk into a glass measuring cup with a spout. Add the vanilla and stir well.

5. **Add the eggs.** Crack 1 egg into a small bowl (if you get any shell in it, see page 5 for tips on easily removing it). Add the egg to the butter mixture. Mix on medium speed for 1 minute. Using a spatula, scrape down the sides of the bowl. Repeat with the remaining egg. Mix for 1 minute. Stop and scrape down the bowl again.

6. **Add the dry ingredients to the wet ingredients.** Pour half the flour mixture into the butter mixture. Mix on low speed for 10 seconds. Add half the milk mixture. Mix for 10 seconds more. Stop the mixer and use the spatula to scrape down the sides of the bowl. Add the remaining flour and milk mixtures, mixing for 10 seconds between each addition. Stop and scrape down the sides of the bowl again. Stir the batter a few more times just until you can't see any flour.

7. **Color the batter.** Evenly divide the batter among 3 small bowls. Add 2 or 3 drops of food coloring to each bowl—one blue, one red, and one green—and stir (use a separate spoon for each color) until the colors are uniform in each bowl.

8. **Fill the pan.** Use a spoon to place 1 scoop of blue batter into each pre-pared muffin cup. Use a second spoon to add a scoop of red batter on top of the blue batter. Use a third spoon to

add the green batter on top. Each cup should be about three-quarters full. Use a toothpick to swirl the colors together gently in a circle.

9. **Bake.** Carefully place the pan onto the center rack of the preheated oven. Bake for 18 to 20 minutes, rotating the pan halfway through baking (use oven mitts!) so your cupcakes bake evenly. The cupcakes are ready when you can press on the top of them with your finger and the cake springs back (ask an adult to help).

10. **Let cool.** Remove the pan from the oven (use oven mitts!) and place on a wire rack. Let the cupcakes cool in the pan for 10 minutes. Once they're cool enough to touch, remove the cupcakes from the pan and transfer them to the wire rack to cool completely, about 1 hour.

11. **Make the frosting.** While the cupcakes are cooling, make the vanilla buttercream following the directions on page 128.

TO DECORATE

12. **Color the frosting.** Add 1 drop of blue food coloring to the frosting and mix well.

13. **Frost the cupcakes.** Once the cupcakes are completely cooled, use a knife, offset spatula, or a piping bag to spread an even layer of frosting on top of each cupcake.

14. **Cut the rainbows.** Using kitchen shears, cut the rainbow candy strips into 4-inch pieces.

15. **Cut the marshmallows.** Using kitchen shears, cut each marshmallow into 4 pieces. Roll each piece between your (clean) palms until round, like clouds.

16. **Assemble the rainbows.** Push one end of the rainbow strip into the frosting on one side of the cupcake, and then push the other end into the other side. Place 3 or 4 marshmallow rounds at the base of each side of the rainbow.

🔄 **Change It Up:** Instead of adding candy rainbows to your cupcakes, decorate them with rainbow icing. Divide your frosting evenly into a few bowls and add a drop of a different color to each one. Add 1 teaspoon of each color of frosting to the top of your cupcakes or swirl them together in a piping bag for a neat rainbow effect.

chapter 5

HOLIDAY IDEAS

Whether you're celebrating love or fireworks, leprechauns or Christmas trees, all 10 of these ideas will help make a special day even sweeter.

Need more photos? Visit my website at Foodlets.com/cupcakes for pictures of each recipe.

BE MY VALENTINE: TWO HEARTS

You can turn any cupcake into a Valentine's Day treat in no time with these two methods for making hearts! All it takes are a couple of special tools you can find online or at baking specialty stores: heart-shaped cookie cutters and ceramic pie weights. And, if pie weights aren't possible, use rolled-up aluminum foil instead.

MAKES	PREP TIME	BAKE TIME	NUT-FREE
12 CUPCAKES	**1** HOUR	**20** MINUTES	

Method 1: Heart-Shaped Cupcakes

1 batch Strawberry Cupcakes (page 23)

1 batch Fruity Buttercream with strawberry jam (page 129)

TOOLS

Standard 12-cup muffin pan
Silicone baking cups
12 ceramic pie weights or aluminum foil balls (about the size of a marble)
Aluminum foil
Knife or offset spatula

1. Preheat the oven. Set the oven to 350°F. Line a muffin pan with paper liners, or grease the inside of each cup with cooking spray or butter (see page 5).

2. Make the heart shapes. Nestle one pie weight or foil ball on the outside of the silicone baking cup to make a dent (the top of the heart). Fold 24 pieces of foil into small rectangles, about the size of a stick of gum. Place the fillers on each side of the cupcake liners, at the bottom of each cupcake, to form a V shape. Your muffin pan should now have 12 heart-shaped cups.

3. Make the cupcakes. Make the strawberry cupcakes following the directions on page 23. You may have some batter left over—just refill the pan after the first batch comes out of the oven and bake a second batch of cupcakes! Let cool completely, about 1 hour.

4. Make the frosting. While the cupcakes are cooling, make the fruity buttercream with strawberry jam following the directions on page 129.

5. Frost the cupcakes. Once the cupcakes are completely cooled, use a knife or offset spatula to spread an even layer of frosting on top of each cupcake.

Method 2: Heart-Topped Cupcakes

FOR THE CUPCAKES

1 batch Strawberry Cupcakes (page 23)

1 batch Fruity Buttercream (page 129)

FOR THE DECORATION

Sprinkles

TOOLS

Knife or offset spatula
Small heart-shaped cookie cutter

TO MAKE THE CUPCAKES AND FROSTING

1. Make the cupcakes. Make the strawberry cupcakes following the directions on page 23. Let cool completely, about 1 hour.

2. Make the frosting. While the cupcakes are cooling, make the fruity buttercream following the directions on page 129.

TO DECORATE

3. Frost the cupcakes. Once the cupcakes are completely cooled, use a knife or offset spatula to spread an even layer of frosting on top of each cupcake, making a mound in the center.

4. Decorate. Place the heart-shaped cookie cutter on top of a frosted cupcake. Pour the sprinkles inside the cookie cutter. Carefully remove the cookie cutter to reveal a heart of sprinkles on top! Repeat with the remaining cupcakes.

Change It Up: Change the cookie cutter—and color of sprinkles—to suit other holidays! For example, use a shamrock with green sprinkles for St. Patrick's Day or a star with red sprinkles for Christmas.

COLOR ME GREEN

What better way to celebrate St. Patty's Day than with green cupcakes? Top these bonnie treats with a chocolate gold coin and you'll have the luck o' the Irish all day long.

| MAKES **12** CUPCAKES | PREP TIME **45** MINUTES | BAKE TIME **20** MINUTES | NUT-FREE |

TOOLS

Standard 12-cup muffin pan
Cupcake liners (optional)
Measuring cups and spoons
Stand mixer fitted with paddle attachment or large bowl and electric beaters
Silicone spatula
Small bowl
#20 ice-cream scoop with spring release
Oven mitts
Wire rack
Knife or offset spatula
Piping bag and large tip (optional)

Change It Up: Do you know what else is festive for St. Patrick's Day? Rainbows! Follow the instructions on page 99 and add 2 or 3 yellow M&Ms for the "gold" at the ends of your rainbows.

FOR THE CUPCAKES

Nonstick cooking spray (optional)
8 tablespoons (1 stick) unsalted butter, at room temperature, plus more for preparing the pan (optional)
1 cup sugar
1½ cups all-purpose flour
1½ teaspoons baking powder
½ teaspoon fine salt
½ cup full-fat plain yogurt
2 teaspoons pure vanilla extract
3 large eggs
2 to 4 drops green food color gel

1 batch Vanilla Buttercream (page 128)

FOR THE DECORATION

12 chocolate gold coins
Green or gold sprinkles

TO MAKE THE CUPCAKES AND FROSTING

1. Preheat the oven. Set the oven to 350°F. Line a muffin pan with paper liners, or grease the inside of each cup with cooking spray or butter (see page 5).

2. Mix the dry ingredients. In the bowl of a stand mixer fitted with the paddle attachment, or a large bowl using electric beaters, combine the sugar, flour, baking powder, and salt. Mix on low speed for 30 seconds.

3. Mix the wet ingredients. Add the butter, yogurt, and vanilla. Mix on medium speed for 30 seconds. Stop the mixer and use a spatula to scrape down the sides of the bowl.

4. Add the eggs. Crack 1 egg into a small bowl (if you get any shell in it, see page 5 for tips on easily removing it). Add the egg to the batter. Mix on medium speed for 30 seconds. Separate the remaining 2 eggs (see page 5, or ask an adult to help you) into 2 small bowls (whites in one, yolks in another). Pour just the yolks into the batter (save the whites for another use). Mix on medium speed for about 30 seconds until the batter is silky smooth. Stop the mixer and use the spatula to scrape down the sides of the bowl. Stir the batter a few more times just until you can't see any flour.

5. Color the batter. Add 2 drops of green coloring to the batter. Using the spatula, stir until well incorporated (if the color isn't dark enough for you, add 2 more drops and stir again).

6. Fill the pan. Using an ice-cream scoop, divide the batter evenly among the prepared cups, filling each about three-quarters full.

7. Bake. Carefully place the pan onto the center rack of the preheated oven. Bake for 18 to 20 minutes, rotating the pan halfway through baking (use oven mitts!) so your cupcakes bake evenly. The cupcakes are ready when you can press on the top of them with your finger and the cake springs back (ask an adult to help).

8. Let cool. Remove the pan from the oven (use oven mitts!) and place on a wire rack. Let the cupcakes cool in the pan for 10 minutes. Once they're cool enough to touch, remove the cupcakes from the pan and transfer them to the wire rack to cool completely, about 1 hour.

9. Make the frosting. While the cupcakes are cooling, make the vanilla buttercream following the directions on page 128.

TO DECORATE

10. Frost the cupcakes. Once the cupcakes are completely cooled, use a knife or offset spatula to spread an even layer of frosting on top of each cupcake, making a mound in the center. Alternatively, ask an adult to fill a piping bag using a large tip. Make a big swirl of frosting on top of each cupcake.

11. Decorate. Place a gold chocolate coin on the top of each frosted cupcake so it's standing upright. Finish with a liberal dusting of sprinkles.

SPRINGTIME BIRD NESTS

Candy eggs in chocolate nests—what could be sweeter? With just a few extra ingredients, you can transform Coconut Cupcakes (page 18) into a decadent scene perfect for spring!

MAKES	PREP TIME	BAKE TIME
12	**1**	**20**
CUPCAKES	HOUR	MINUTES

FOR THE CUPCAKES

1 batch Coconut Cupcakes (page 18)

¼ cup chocolate chips

8 ounces (1 brick) full-fat cream cheese, at room temperature

8 tablespoons (1 stick) unsalted butter, at room temperature

1 teaspoon pure vanilla extract

½ teaspoon pure almond extract

1 cup sweetened finely shredded coconut

FOR THE DECORATION

Egg-shaped candies (jellybeans or mini eggs), for decorating

TOOLS

Microwave-safe bowl

Spoon

Stand mixer fitted with paddle attachment or large bowl and electric beaters

#20 ice-cream scoop with spring release

TO MAKE THE CUPCAKES AND FROSTING

1. Make the cupcakes. Make the coconut cupcakes following the directions on page 18. Let cool completely, about 1 hour.

2. Make the frosting. In a microwave-safe bowl, melt the chocolate chips on High power in 20-second increments, stirring between each, until smooth. In the bowl of a stand mixer fitted with the paddle attachment, or a large bowl using electric beaters, cream together the cream cheese, butter, vanilla, and almond extract on medium speed for about 2 minutes until smooth. Add the melted chocolate and mix until well incorporated. Add the coconut and mix well.

TO DECORATE

3. Frost the cupcakes. Using an ice-cream scoop or big spoon, add a large mound of frosting to the top of each cupcake.

4. Make the nests. Using the back of a spoon, flatten the center of each mound of frosting to form a "nest." Fill each "nest" with candy eggs.

Change It Up: Want to make the nests more robust? Frost the cupcakes with Chocolate Buttercream (page 135). In a microwave-safe bowl, melt ½ cup of chocolate chips (follow the directions in step 2). Using a silicone spatula, gently stir 1 cup of crispy chow mein noodles into the melted chocolate. Drop mounds of the chocolate-noodle mixture onto a parchment paper–lined baking sheet. Using the back of a spoon, press down on the center of each mound to form a "nest." Fill each "nest" with candy eggs. Let cool completely. Arrange on top of each frosted cupcake.

FLUFFY LITTLE LAMBS

You can make the cutest lamb faces using mini marshmallows! Ask an adult to help you make the first one, if needed, so you have a guide to follow. You'll have a flock of little lambs on a platter in minutes.

MAKES **12** CUPCAKES	PREP TIME **1½** HOURS	BAKE TIME **20** MINUTES	NUT-FREE

FOR THE CUPCAKES

1 batch Lemon Cupcakes (page 35)

1 batch Vanilla Buttercream (page 128)

FOR THE DECORATIONS

Mini marshmallows
Pink glitter sprinkles
Black writing icing
Pink jellybeans

TOOLS

Knife or offset spatula
Small plate
Kitchen shears

TO MAKE THE CUPCAKES AND FROSTING

1. Make the cupcakes. Make the lemon cupcakes following the directions on page 35. Let cool completely, about 1 hour.

2. Make the frosting. While the cupcakes are cooling, make the vanilla buttercream following the directions on page 128.

TO DECORATE

3. Frost the cupcakes. Once the cupcakes are completely cooled, use a knife or offset spatula to spread an even layer of frosting on top of each cupcake, making a mound in the center.

4. Make the lamb's face. Arrange a ring of marshmallows, round-side up, side by side, all the way around the edge of each cupcake. Add a second row of marshmallows inside the outer ring, using 4 mini marshmallows (this is the "wool" around the lamb's face).

5. Make the ears. Pour the pink sprinkles onto a small plate. Using kitchen shears, cut 1 mini marshmallow in half diagonally. Dip the cut side into the pink sprinkles to make "ears." Place one "ear" on each side of the second row. Repeat with the remaining cupcakes.

6. Draw the face. Using the black icing, draw 2 curves for eyes plus a mouth on the top of each cupcake. Finish the face with a pink jellybean in the middle for a nose.

Ask an Adult: Have an adult show you how to hold and cut the marshmallow "ears" before trying on your own. They'll be sticky.

Change It Up: Do you know what else is white and fluffy besides lambs? Popcorn! To make movie popcorn cupcakes, shop for red and white cupcake liners (popcorn bags!) and bake your cupcakes according to the instructions. When cool, use an ice-cream scoop to add lots of frosting on top of each cupcake (you might need a double batch!). Stick mini marshmallows to every possible surface of the frosting. When you're done, it'll look like popcorn bursting up and out of a popcorn bag.

RED, WHITE & BLUE FOR YOU

Use red, white, and blue M&Ms to make Independence Day even sweeter. Create a pattern of colorful rings or top each cupcake with a quirky mix of colors. If you prefer, use one color of M&Ms for each cupcake.

MAKES	PREP TIME	BAKE TIME	
12 CUPCAKES	**45** MINUTES	**20** MINUTES	**NUT-FREE**

FOR THE CUPCAKES

1 batch Red Velvet Cupcakes (page 28)

1 batch Cream Cheese Frosting (page 131)

FOR THE DECORATION

Red, white, and blue M&Ms

TOOLS

Knife or offset spatula

TO MAKE THE CUPCAKES AND FROSTING

1. **Make the cupcakes.** Make the red velvet cupcakes following the directions on page 28. Let cool completely, about 1 hour.

2. **Make the frosting.** While the cupcakes are cooling, make the cream cheese frosting following the directions on page 131.

TO DECORATE

3. **Frost the cupcakes.** Once the cupcakes are completely cooled, use a knife or offset spatula to spread an even layer of frosting on top of each cupcake.

4. **Sort the M&Ms.** Sort the red, white, and blue M&Ms into separate piles.

5. **Decorate.** Place 3 blue M&Ms in the center of each cupcake, with the edges tucked into the frosting. Place a ring of red M&Ms around the blue. Repeat with the white M&Ms, then again with blue, and red, until the cupcake is completely covered.

⭐ **Star Baker:** Did you know M&Ms used to come in cardboard tubes? The tubes were easy to pour, plus they protected the candies. That was especially important for soldiers in World War II who enjoyed M&Ms as part of their rations.

YUMMY MUMMIES

You'll need a piping bag to make these mummy cupcakes, but trust me, the result is worth the effort! With their fall flavors, carrot cake cupcakes are my favorite place to start, but use any cupcake flavor you love.

MAKES **12** CUPCAKES	PREP TIME **1** HOUR	BAKE TIME **20** MINUTES	NUT-FREE

FOR THE CUPCAKES

1 batch Carrot Cake Cupcakes (page 37)

1 batch Cream Cheese Frosting (page 131)

FOR THE DECORATION

Candy eyeballs

Sprinkles

TOOLS

Pastry bag fitted with flat tip

TO MAKE THE CUPCAKES AND FROSTING

1. **Make the cupcakes.** Make the carrot cake cupcakes following the directions on page 37. Let cool completely, about 1 hour.

2. **Make the frosting.** While the cupcakes are cooling, make the cream cheese frosting following the directions on page 131.

TO DECORATE

3. **Decorate.** Transfer the frosting to a pastry bag fitted with the flat tip (ask an adult to help, if needed). Place 2 eyeballs on the cupcakes, near the top. To make the mummy's wrap, squeeze the frosting back and forth to create "bandage" lines on the tops of each cupcake, leaving space around the eyeballs. Finish with a dusting of sprinkles.

Change It Up: Want to make ghosts instead? Use a large round tip in your piping bag. Pipe a swirly mound on each cupcake, finishing with a pointed tip. Arrange 2 candy eyes on one side of each mound. Ta-da! You have 12 ghosts.

WICKED WITCH HATS

These chocolatey witch hats come together with just a couple of store-bought ingredients. Ask an adult to help set up the first one and you'll be on your way to a dozen delicious Halloween treats. See page 102 for photos!

MAKES **12** CUPCAKES

PREP TIME **1** HOUR

BAKE TIME **20** MINUTES

NUT-FREE

FOR THE CUPCAKES

1 batch Chocolate Cupcakes (page 31)
1 batch Vanilla Buttercream (page 128)

FOR THE DECORATION

Green and orange food coloring gel
6 Oreo cookies
12 chocolate kisses, unwrapped
Sprinkles

TOOLS

Small bowl
Large bowl
Spoons
Knife or offset spatula

TO MAKE THE CUPCAKES AND FROSTING

1. Make the cupcakes. Make the chocolate cupcakes following the directions on page 31. Let cool completely, about 1 hour.

2. Make the frosting. While the cupcakes are cooling, make the vanilla buttercream following the directions on page 128.

TO DECORATE

3. Color the frosting. Transfer ½ cup of frosting to a small bowl. Add green food coloring gel to the remaining (large) bowl of frosting a bit at a time until you reach your desired shade. To the small bowl, stir in orange food coloring gel a bit at a time until you reach your desired shade. Stir each until smooth.

4. Make the hats. Twist open an Oreo and scrape off the white filling (save the filling in a small container to sprinkle on top of chocolate ice cream another time). On the writing-side of each cookie top, place 1 teaspoon of orange frosting. Top with an unwrapped kiss, pressing it down so the orange frosting forms a rim around the chocolate. Add a few sprinkles to the top of the orange frosting. Repeat until you have 12 hats.

5. Frost the cupcakes. Once the cupcakes are completely cooled, use a knife or offset spatula to spread an even layer of green frosting on top of each cupcake.

6. Add the hats. Perch a hat on top of each frosted cupcake.

★ Star Baker: For the ultimate effect, use green paper cupcake liners when baking the cupcakes and fill the cupcakes with Boston cream filling (see Boston Cream Cupcakes with Chocolate Glaze, page 49) colored with green food coloring gel.

HORNS OF PLENTY TO BE THANKFUL FOR

Ever heard of a cornucopia? It's a horn overflowing with fruits, symbolizing an incredible bounty. Thanksgiving will be even more delicious with these gorgeous pumpkin and chocolate chip cornucopia cupcakes!

MAKES **12** CUPCAKES	PREP TIME **45** MINUTES	BAKE TIME **20** MINUTES	NUT-FREE

FOR THE CUPCAKES

Nonstick cooking spray, or unsalted butter for preparing the pan (optional)

⅔ cup packed light brown sugar

½ cup olive oil

1 cup pure pumpkin puree (about half a 15-ounce can)

½ cup full-fat sour cream

2 large eggs

1½ cups all-purpose flour

2 teaspoons ground cinnamon

1½ teaspoons pumpkin pie spice, or 1 teaspoon ground ginger plus ½ teaspoon ground nutmeg

2 teaspoons baking powder

1 teaspoon baking soda

½ teaspoon fine salt

1 cup mini chocolate chips

1 batch Cream Cheese Frosting (page 131)

FOR THE DECORATION

Bugles corn snacks

Runts fruit-shaped candies

Pumpkin-shaped candies

TOOLS

Standard 12-cup muffin pan

Cupcake liners (optional)

Measuring cups and spoons

Stand mixer fitted with paddle attachment or large bowl and electric beaters

Small bowl

Silicone spatula

Sifter

#20 ice-cream scoop with spring release

Oven mitts

Wire rack

Knife or offset spatula

TO MAKE THE CUPCAKES AND FROSTING

1. **Preheat the oven.** Set the oven to 350°F. Line a muffin pan with paper liners, or grease the inside of each cup with cooking spray or butter (see page 5).

2. **Mix the wet ingredients.** In the bowl of a stand mixer fitted with the paddle attachment, or a large bowl using electric beaters, combine the brown sugar, oil, pumpkin, and sour cream. Mix on medium speed for about 2 minutes until fluffy.

3. **Add the eggs.** Crack 1 egg into a small bowl (if you get any shell in it, see page 5 for tips on easily removing it). Add the egg to the pumpkin mixture. Mix on medium speed for 1 minute. Using the spatula, scrape down the sides of the bowl. Repeat with the remaining egg.

4. **Sift the dry ingredients.** Remove the bowl from the mixer stand. Place a sifter over the bowl. Add the flour, cinnamon, pumpkin pie spice, baking powder, baking soda, and salt to the sifter. Gently shake the sifter to move all the ingredients into the bowl. Using the spatula, gently fold (stir down, over, and up again, repeating in a circle) the flour mixture into the pumpkin mixture. Fold in the mini chocolate chips.

5. **Fill the pan.** Using an ice-cream scoop, divide the batter evenly among the prepared cups, filling each about three-quarters full.

6. **Bake.** Carefully place the pan onto the center rack of the preheated oven. Bake for 18 to 20 minutes, rotating the pan halfway through baking (use oven mitts!) so your cupcakes bake evenly. The cupcakes are ready when you can press on the top of them with your finger and the cake springs back (ask an adult to help).

7. **Let cool.** Remove the pan from the oven (use oven mitts!) and place on a wire rack. Let the cupcakes cool in the pan for 10 minutes. Once they're cool enough to touch, remove the cupcakes from the pan and transfer them to the wire rack to cool completely, about 1 hour.

CONTINUED ON NEXT PAGE

8. **Make the frosting.** While the cupcakes are cooling, make the cream cheese frosting following the directions on page 131.

TO DECORATE

9. **Frost the cupcakes.** Once the cupcakes are completely cooled, use a knife or offset spatula to spread an even layer of frosting on top of each cupcake.

10. **Decorate.** To the top of each cupcake, just off-center, arrange a Bugle snack on its side as the cornucopia. Place a little pile of candy fruit inside the horn and next to it. Finish by nestling a pumpkin candy in with the fruit.

Change It Up: Want another fun idea for fall? Cut leaf shapes from pie dough using a cookie cutter (or ask an adult to help with a knife) and place on a parchment paper–lined baking sheet. Dust with cinnamon sugar and bake at 400°F for about 8 minutes. Arrange the leaves on top of frosted cupcakes.

GINGERBREAD CUPCAKES
DECORATED FOUR WAYS

Move over, tiny houses—this gingerbread recipe makes fluffy cupcakes bursting with holiday flavor! And that's just the beginning. With just a handful of M&Ms you can decorate your cupcakes in four adorable ways: a jumble of Christmas lights, a snowman's smiling face, the Star of David, or a Christmas tree.

MAKES	PREP TIME	BAKE TIME	
12 CUPCAKES	**1** HOUR	**20** MINUTES	NUT-FREE

⭐ **Star Baker:** There's not a single egg in this recipe! The acid in molasses works with baking soda to create all the air bubbles you need for the cupcakes to rise.

FOR THE CUPCAKES

Nonstick cooking spray (optional)

8 tablespoons (1 stick) unsalted butter, melted, plus more for preparing the pan (optional)

1 cup molasses

1 cup full-fat sour cream

Grated zest of 1 orange

2⅓ cups all-purpose flour

2 teaspoons ground ginger

1 teaspoon baking soda

1 teaspoon ground cinnamon

½ teaspoon fine salt

¼ teaspoon ground cloves

2 tablespoons dried candied ginger, minced

1 batch Vanilla Buttercream (page 128)

FOR THE DECORATION

1 (1-ounce) tube black writing icing (sometimes called cookie icing)

M&Ms

TOOLS

Zester or box grater (use the small holes)

Standard 12-cup muffin pan

Cupcake liners (optional)

Measuring cups and spoons

CONTINUED ON NEXT PAGE

Stand mixer fitted with paddle attachment or large bowl and electric beaters

Sifter

Silicone spatula

#20 ice-cream scoop with spring release

Oven mitts

Wire rack

Knife or offset spatula

TO MAKE THE CUPCAKES AND FROSTING

1. Preheat the oven. Set the oven to 350°F. Line a muffin pan with paper liners, or grease the inside of each cup with cooking spray or butter (see page 5).

2. Mix the wet ingredients. In the bowl of a stand mixer fitted with the paddle attachment, or a large bowl using electric beaters, combine the melted butter and molasses. Mix on low speed for about 20 seconds until incorporated. Add the sour cream and orange zest and mix for 20 seconds more.

3. Sift the dry ingredients. Remove the bowl from the mixer stand. Place a sifter over the bowl. Add the flour, ginger, baking soda, cinnamon, salt, and cloves to the sifter. Gently shake the sifter to move all the ingredients into the bowl.

Return the bowl to the stand and mix on low speed for 20 seconds, just until incorporated. Using a spatula, scrape down the sides of the bowl. Stir the batter a few more times just until you can't see any flour. Using a spatula, fold (stir down, over, and up again, repeating in a circle) in the candied ginger.

4. Fill the pan. Using an ice-cream scoop, divide the batter evenly among the prepared cups, filling each about three-quarters full.

5. Bake. Carefully place the pan onto the center rack of the preheated oven. Bake for 18 to 20 minutes, rotating the pan halfway through baking (use oven mitts!) so your cupcakes bake evenly. The cupcakes are ready when you can press on the top of them with your finger and the cake springs back (ask an adult to help).

6. Let cool. Remove the pan from the oven (use oven mitts!) and place on a wire rack. Let the cupcakes cool in the pan for 10 minutes. Once they're cool enough to touch, remove the cupcakes from the pan and transfer them to the wire rack to cool completely, about 1 hour.

7. Make the frosting. While the cupcakes are cooling, make the vanilla buttercream following the directions on page 128.

TO MAKE THE CHRISTMAS LIGHT JUMBLE

1. Frost the cupcakes. Once the cupcakes are completely cooled, use a knife or offset spatula to spread an even layer of frosting on top of each cupcake, making a mound in the center.

2. Draw the "cord." Squeeze the tube of black icing to draw a curved line across each cupcake (embellish with a loop or two!).

3. Add the "lights." Arrange 7 or 8 M&Ms on their sides, spaced evenly along the black cord, to form the Christmas "lights."

TO MAKE THE SNOWMAN FACE

1. Frost the cupcakes. Once the cupcakes are completely cooled, use a knife or offset spatula to spread an even layer of frosting on top of each cupcake, making a mound in the center.

2. Sort the M&MS by color. Set aside the brown and orange M&Ms.

3. Make the face. For the eyes, arrange two brown M&Ms at the top of your frosted cupcakes. Add a smile using 4 or 5 brown M&Ms. To make the nose, press 1 orange M&M on its side in the middle of the face.

TO MAKE THE STAR OF DAVID

1. Frost the cupcakes. Once the cupcakes are completely cooled, use a knife or offset spatula to spread an even layer of frosting on top of each cupcake, making a mound in the center.

2. Sort the M&MS by color. Set aside all the blue M&Ms.

3. Make the star. Arrange blue M&Ms on their sides to form a Star of David on the top of each cupcake.

TO MAKE THE CHRISTMAS TREE

1. Frost the cupcakes. Once the cupcakes are completely cooled, use a knife or offset spatula to spread an even layer of frosting on top of each cupcake, making a mound in the center.

2. Sort the M&MS by color. Set aside all the green, brown, and yellow M&Ms.

3. Make the tree. Arrange green M&Ms on their sides to form a "tree": 1 at the top, 2 in the next layer, 3, then 4. To make the "trunk," place 1 brown M&M on its side at the bottom of the triangle. To make the "star," perch 1 yellow M&M at the very top of the triangle.

GOING, GOING, GONE SNOWMEN

With a marshmallow and food-safe marker, make melting snowmen the showcase of your holiday season. Bonus: With a spray of whipped cream as the "body," this technique works atop a mug of hot chocolate, too! Just be quick, because your snowmen really will melt . . .

MAKES **12** **CUPCAKES**

PREP TIME **1½** **HOURS**

BAKE TIME **20** **MINUTES**

NUT-FREE

FOR THE CUPCAKES

1 batch Vanilla Cupcakes (page 39)

1 batch Vanilla Buttercream (page 128)

FOR THE DECORATION

Marshmallows (regular size, not mini)

Orange sprinkles, or orange chewy candies

Pretzel sticks

M&Ms

TOOLS

Food-safe marker

Piping bag fitted with large round tip

TO MAKE THE CUPCAKES AND FROSTING

1. Make the cupcakes. Make the vanilla cupcakes following the directions on page 39. Let cool completely, about 1 hour.

2. Make the frosting. While the cupcakes are cooling, make the vanilla buttercream following the directions on page 128.

CONTINUED ON NEXT PAGE

TO DECORATE

3. Make the snowman's head. Using the marker, draw eyes and a smile on the flat round side of each marshmallow. To make the nose, pierce each marshmallow with an orange sprinkle (or ask an adult to help cut a chewy orange candy into a nose shape).

4. Frost the cupcakes. Once the cupcakes are completely cooled, transfer the frosting to a piping bag with a large round tip (ask an adult to help, if needed) and squeeze mounds of frosting onto each cupcake.

5. Decorate. Arrange 1 snowman's head on top of each frosted cupcake. Poke a pretzel stick into each side of the frosting as the arms. Add the "buttons" by arranging 2 M&Ms down the front of each snowman.

Change It Up: Want another easy-peasy holiday idea? Place candy canes in a resealable bag, crush with a rolling pin, and sprinkle crushed candy canes on top of vanilla cupcakes with vanilla frosting.

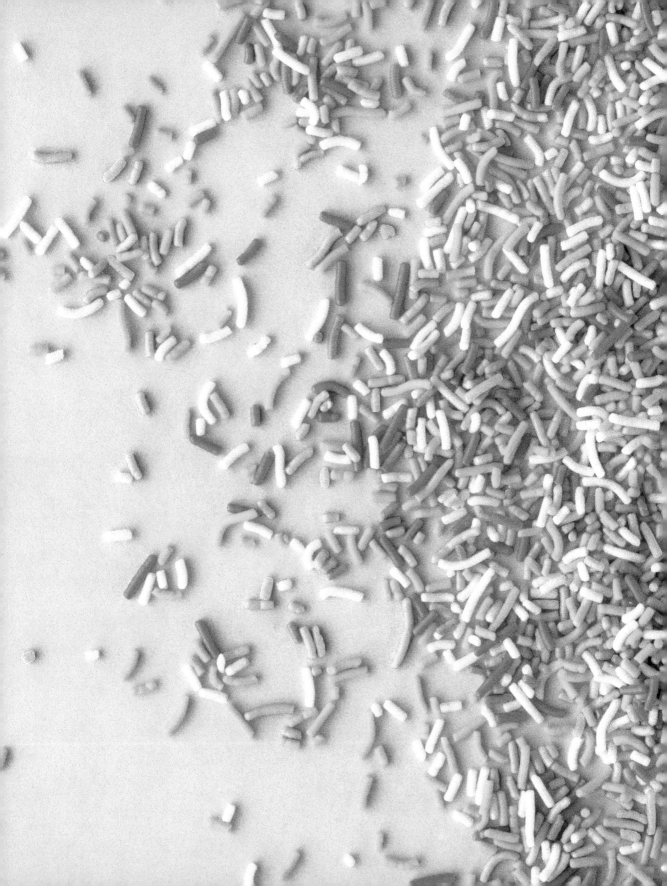

chapter 6
FROSTINGS

There are so many ways to top your delicious cupcakes! From fluffy buttercream to smooth glaze and even s'mores, you'll find 10 techniques right here.

VANILLA BUTTERCREAM

This classic vanilla buttercream recipe is the base for many ideas in this book. Color it, decorate it, or just pile it high. Of all the vanilla frostings out there, this one is the most reliably delicious.

MAKES	PREP TIME	
3 CUPS	**15** MINUTES	**NUT-FREE**

12 tablespoons (1½ sticks) unsalted butter, at room temperature

3 cups powdered sugar

⅛ teaspoon fine salt

2 teaspoons pure vanilla extract

2 tablespoons whole milk

1. **Cream the butter.** In the bowl of a stand mixer fitted with the paddle attachment, or a large bowl using electric beaters, combine the butter, powdered sugar, and salt. Mix on low speed for about 30 seconds until the sugar is incorporated. Using a spatula, scrape down the sides of the bowl.

2. **Add the wet ingredients.** Add the vanilla and mix on medium speed for about 3 minutes until creamy, stopping partway through to scrape down the sides of the bowl with a spatula. Add the milk and mix for about 1 minute more until fluffy.

Change It Up: Make peppermint frosting: Substitute ¼ teaspoon of pure peppermint extract for the vanilla in step 3. Top frosted cupcakes with crushed candy canes or an unwrapped chocolate mint candy.

FRUITY BUTTERCREAM

With the tang of orange marmalade, this buttercream is perfect on our Creamy Dreamy Orange Cupcakes (page 61), but you can replace the marmalade with almost any jam, including strawberry for our Valentine's Day cupcakes (page 104). Want more ideas? Try raspberry, blackberry, or even lemon curd. Consider adding 1 or 2 drops of food coloring to give a hint of the flavor you're serving: red plus yellow for orange, red for strawberry, blue for blackberry.

MAKES ABOUT	PREP TIME	
2 CUPS	**15** MINUTES	**NUT-FREE**

★ **Star Baker:**
Have you ever wondered if cream cheese is real cheese? The answer is yes! Although most cheese is made from milk alone, cream cheese is also made with cream. That's where it gets the name.

4 ounces (½ brick) full-fat cream cheese
4 tablespoons (½ stick) unsalted butter, at room temperature
2 cups powdered sugar
¼ cup orange marmalade, or strawberry, raspberry, or blackberry jam
Food coloring (optional)

1. **Cream the butter.** In the bowl of a stand mixer fitted with the paddle attachment, or a large bowl using electric beaters, combine the cream cheese and butter. Mix on medium-high speed for about 2 minutes until smooth.

2. **Add the sugar.** Add the powdered sugar. Mix on low speed for about 30 seconds until well incorporated.

3. **Add the flavoring.** One tablespoon at a time, add the marmalade, mixing after each addition until the mixture is soft enough to mix well but not too runny to spread on cupcakes (ask an adult to help, if needed). Once at the desired consistency, mix on high speed for about 2 minutes until fluffy.

WHIPPED CREAM FROSTING

The trouble with plain whipped cream is that, although it's delicious, it usually runs everywhere once it warms up. That's why this recipe is genius: You get all the light and airy flavor of whipped cream in a frosting that's stable enough to hold up for your favorite cupcakes. Bonus: You can easily transform this frosting into Whipped Butterbeer Frosting (see Star Baker tip) for our Butterbeer Cupcakes (page 71).

MAKES 2 CUPS

PREP TIME 15 MINUTES

NUT-FREE

1 cup heavy (whipping) cream
2 tablespoons powdered sugar
½ (3.4-ounce) package instant vanilla pudding

1. Whip the cream. In the bowl of a stand mixer fitted with the whisk attachment, or a large bowl using electric beaters, beat the cream on medium-high speed for 6 to 7 minutes until "soft peaks" form. When you tilt the whisk up, the cream should stick to it like a fluffy cloud.

2. Add the sugar. Add the powdered sugar and continue beating for 30 seconds.

3. Add the flavoring and thickener. Add the pudding mix. Beat on medium speed for 30 seconds, or just until the frosting starts to thicken. Stop the mixer and use a silicone spatula to scrape down the sides and bottom of the bowl. Beat for 10 seconds more to incorporate any remaining pudding mix.

★ **Star Baker:** Make whipped butterbeer frosting by substituting butterscotch instant pudding for the vanilla pudding and adding 2 teaspoons of imitation butter extract in step 3. For the most glamorous look, use a pastry bag fitted with a large tip to pile the frosting high on top of each cupcake.

CREAM CHEESE FROSTING

There isn't a more perfect topping for Carrot Cake Cupcakes (page 37) than cream cheese frosting. Rich and creamy with just the right amount of zing, it's also a favorite on top of Red Velvet Cupcakes (page 28). Plus, you can add coconut to make Cream Cheese–Coconut Frosting for our incredible Coconut Cupcakes (page 18).

MAKES	PREP TIME	NUT-FREE
2 CUPS	**15** MINUTES	

4 tablespoons (½ stick) unsalted butter, at room temperature

6 ounces (almost 1 full brick) full-fat cream cheese, at room temperature

1 teaspoon pure vanilla extract

⅛ teaspoon fine salt

2 cups powdered sugar

1. Cream the butter. In the bowl of a stand mixer fitted with the paddle attachment, or a large bowl using electric beaters, combine the butter and cream cheese. Mix on medium speed for 30 seconds until well combined. Using a spatula, scrape down the sides of the bowl. Add the vanilla and salt. Mix on medium speed for about 2 minutes until creamy.

2. Add the sugar. Add the powdered sugar. Mix on low speed for about 30 seconds just until the powdered sugar is incorporated. Mix on high speed for about 2 minutes until thick and fluffy.

Change It Up: Make cream cheese-coconut frosting. Add 1 cup of sweetened coconut in step 2. Or, for a fall-flavored treat, add ½ teaspoon of ground cinnamon to the powdered sugar before mixing it in. It's perfect for Cinnamon Spice Cupcakes with Apple Pie Filling (page 58) or Pumpkin Cupcakes (page 21).

PEANUT BUTTER FROSTING

Thick and rich, this fluffy frosting is my absolute favorite way to serve a Chocolate Cupcake (page 31). Want to go extra? Add a chopped-up peanut butter cup on top.

MAKES ABOUT **2** CUPS

PREP TIME **15** MINUTES

8 tablespoons (1 stick) unsalted butter, at room temperature

1 cup creamy peanut butter (not "natural")

2 cups powdered sugar

3 tablespoons whole milk

1. **Cream the butter and peanut butter.** In the bowl of a stand mixer fitted with the paddle attachment, or a large bowl using electric beaters, combine the butter and peanut butter. Mix on medium-high speed for about 2 minutes until smooth.

2. **Add the sugar.** Add the powdered sugar. Mix on low speed for about 30 seconds just until the powdered sugar is incorporated.

3. **Add the liquid.** Add the milk, 1 tablespoon at a time, mixing after each addition until the mixture is soft enough to mix well but not too runny to spread on cupcakes (ask an adult to help, if needed). Mix on high speed for about 2 minutes until fluffy.

★ Star Baker: I love the taste of natural peanut butter (with oil you mix in yourself), but you need the consistency of regular peanut butter for this recipe to work.

LEMON GLAZE

This super-simple glaze comes together with only three ingredients! For added flair, zest the lemons and sprinkle those bright yellow pieces on top of your glaze (ask an adult to help you with the zesting, if needed). Substitute orange juice for the lemon juice and get a whole new flavor!

1½ cups powdered sugar

3 tablespoons unsalted butter, at room temperature

3 teaspoons freshly squeezed lemon juice

Make the glaze. In a medium bowl, combine the powdered sugar, butter, and lemon juice. Using a whisk or a fork, stir until smooth.

🏆 **Super Baker:** You can make this glaze up to 1 week ahead. Just keep it in the refrigerator in an airtight container. When you're ready to use it, remove from the refrigerator and let warm to room temperature for at least 2 hours.

MAKES	PREP TIME	
1 CUP	**15** MINUTES	**NUT-FREE**

CHOCOLATE GLAZE

Get ready for a super-smooth topping that works as well on cupcakes as it does on full-size cakes! Use a spoon to pour a little on top and let the gooey chocolate do the rest, sliding right into place.

MAKES 3/4 CUP

PREP TIME 15 MINUTES

NUT-FREE

½ cup semisweet chocolate chips
3 tablespoons unsalted butter

1. **Melt the chocolate.** Place the chocolate chips in a microwave-safe bowl. Heat on High power in 20-second intervals, stirring between each, until melted.

2. **Finish the glaze.** While the chocolate is still hot, add the butter to the bowl. Using a silicone spatula, stir until the mixture is liquefied and smooth. Set aside to cool for about 10 minutes before using.

Ask an Adult: Get help using the microwave and stirring the warm chocolate.

CHOCOLATE BUTTERCREAM

Rich and creamy with two kinds of chocolate, this buttercream is always a crowd-pleaser.

MAKES	PREP TIME	
2	**15**	**NUT-FREE**
CUPS	MINUTES	

★ **Star Baker:** Want an even easier recipe? Combine 1 cup of chocolate chips (melted and cooled slightly, see steps 1 and 2) with 1 cup of full-fat Greek yogurt. Mix well and you're done. The result is super tangy and not too sweet.

4 ounces semisweet chocolate

8 tablespoons (1 stick) unsalted butter, at room temperature

2 cups powdered sugar

2 tablespoons unsweetened cocoa powder

2 tablespoons whole milk

1 teaspoon pure vanilla extract

1. Melt the chocolate. Place the chocolate in a microwave-safe bowl. Heat on High power in 20-second intervals, stirring between each, until melted. (Ask an adult to help, if needed.)

2. Mix the ingredients. Put the melted chocolate in the bowl of a stand mixer fitted with the paddle attachment, or a large bowl using electric beaters. Turn the mixer on low speed for 5 seconds to cool the chocolate. Add the butter, powdered sugar, cocoa powder, milk, and vanilla. Mix on low speed for about 30 seconds just until the powdered sugar and cocoa powder are incorporated. Increase the speed to high and mix for about 3 minutes until fluffy.

CHOCOLATE-HAZELNUT FROSTING

There's no better topping for our Chocolate-Hazelnut Cupcakes Inside and Out (page 44)! Rich, creamy, and downright dreamy, you need a little extra sugar for this recipe to reach the desired consistency. Once blended, your frosting will be thick enough to spread perfectly *and* hold a chocolate perched on top.

MAKES ABOUT	PREP TIME
4 CUPS	**15** MINUTES

8 tablespoons (1 stick) unsalted butter, at room temperature

4 cups powdered sugar, divided

4 tablespoons whole milk, divided

1 tablespoon unsweetened cocoa powder

½ cup chocolate-hazelnut spread (such as Nutella)

1. Cream the butter. In the bowl of a stand mixer fitted with the paddle attachment, or a large bowl using electric beaters, cream the butter on medium speed for about 2 minutes until fluffy.

2. Add the sugar. Add 2 cups of powdered sugar plus 2 tablespoons of milk. Mix on low speed for about 30 seconds until incorporated.

3. Mix the ingredients. Add the remaining 2 cups of powdered sugar, the cocoa powder, remaining 2 tablespoons of milk, and the chocolate-hazelnut spread. Mix for about 2 minutes until fluffy.

★ **Star Baker:** Using an ice-cream scoop, apply a big scoop of frosting to a cupcake. Using a knife or offset spatula, smooth the top and the edges. Decorate with an unwrapped chocolate ball on top.

S'MORES ON TOP

When I don't have time to make frosting for cupcakes, this is my go-to trick for a treat everyone loves—every time. No mixing required. All you need are baked cupcakes and the ingredients for s'mores: marshmallows, graham crackers, and chocolate bars.

| MAKES TOPPING FOR **12** CUPCAKES | PREP TIME **10** MINUTES | NUT-FREE |

12 regular marshmallows

3 graham crackers, each broken into 4 pieces

1 chocolate bar, broken into 12 pieces

1. Preheat the oven. Preheat the broiler (ask an adult to help).

2. Broil the marshmallow topping. Top each baked cupcake (leave them in the muffin pan) with 1 marshmallow. Place the pan under the broiler for about 1 minute until the marshmallows melt and turn golden on top. (Watch them carefully to prevent burning and ask an adult to help.) Using oven mitts, very carefully remove the pan from the oven.

3. Finish the decoration. Working quickly (and carefully), poke a graham cracker and chocolate piece into the melty marshmallow at an angle. Let cool slightly before serving.

Change It Up: Use flavored (or colored) marshmallows, or use a candy bar with crunchy bits or a gooey filling.

index

acknowledgments

Thank you so much to Laura Apperson and the team at Callisto for helping with every single step of this book!

I'm so grateful to the readers of Foodlets.com, who've tested recipes, given feedback, and, most of all, shared their stories and encouragement over the years. What luck to have such a beautiful community of moms from every corner of the world.

And closer to home, thank you to Gina Rhoades and Andrea Sterling for testing these recipes. Your input makes all the difference! For both of you, plus my mom, Judy Olsen, Mary Curley, Lori Kirsten, Aurora Benton, Katharine Berkowski, Leigh Fickling, and Beth Lundberg, how can I thank you enough for supporting me through every phase, every new idea, every milestone? You make it all seem more doable—and so much fun.

Colleen Chrzanowski Light, your photos of the kids and me are breathtaking. Thank you for sharing your talent with me, and the world.

None of this would be possible without my husband, Paul, holding down the fort while I chase this little dream.

Most of all, I can't believe how lucky I am to have four kids who teach me how to be better at living fully every day. Their hugs, squeals, and prayers ("Thank you, God, that Mommy made this yummy dinner") are more than anything I've ever hoped for. Without Phoebe, Estelle, George, and Violet, there would be no cookbooks, no Foodlets.com, and my heart would never be half as full.

about the author

Charity Curley Mathews is the author of four cookbooks for kids including *Super Simple Baking for Kids*, *Kid Chef Junior Bakes*, and *Pizza School*. As a family food writer and speaker, she's been featured on FoodNetwork.com, Epicurious, Huffington Post, ABC 11-TV, *News of Orange County*, and many other outlets.

She's the founder of Foodlets.com, a website full of shortcut recipes packed with fresh ingredients kids love. Every idea is kid tested and doable for even the busiest families.

She lives in North Carolina with her husband, Paul, and their four children on a small farm, currently home to two Lab rescues, two bunnies, and seven chickens.

Printed in the USA
CPSIA information can be obtained
at www.ICGtesting.com
JSHW071348200823
46850JS00004BA/27

9 781647 392697